School Refusal

Parent, Adolescent and Child Training Skills 2
Series Editor: Martin Herbert

School Refusal

by
David Heyne and Stephanie Rollings
(with Neville King and Bruce Tonge)

Series Editor
Martin Herbert

BPS Blackwell

350 Main Street, Malden, MA 02148-5018, USA
108 Cowley Road, Oxford OX4 1JF, UK
550 Swanston Street, Carlton South, Melbourne, Victoria 3053, Australia
Kurfürstendamm 57, 10707 Berlin, Germany

First published 2002 by The British Psychological Society
and Blackwell Publishing Ltd
Reprinted 2003

Library of Congress Cataloging-in-Publication Data has been applied for

ISBN 1 85433 356 9 (paperback)

A catalogue record for this title is available from the British Library.

Set in Lapidary
by Ralph J. Footring, Derby

For further information on
Blackwell Publishing, visit our website:
http://www.blackwellpublishing.com

Contents

School refusal

Introduction

Difficulties with school attendance can jeopardize a young person's development, cause distress for families and present a considerable challenge for
education, mental health and welfare staff. This guide draws on our clinical
experience and research findings from the Monash Medical Centre School
Refusal Clinic. It provides a brief overview of the field before moving on to
the process, measures and issues in conducting an efficient yet clinically
useful assessment. Throughout, we provide examples of how the strategies
might be applied.

Aims

The aims of this guide are:

➢ to distinguish between school refusal and other forms of school attendance problems;
➢ to assist practitioners with the development of an intervention plan for
  school refusal;
➢ to provide resources useful in the assessment and management of school
  refusal.

Objectives

Having read this book, it is anticipated that you would be able:

➢ to discriminate between types of school attendance problems;
➢ to assess efficiently causative and maintenance factors in school refusal;
➢ confidently to select intervention strategies relevant to school refusers;
➢ additionally to select strategies relevant to working with school refusers'
  parents;
➢ to respond creatively to the challenges of addressing school refusal from
  within the school environment;
➢ to pursue further information pertinent to the assessment and management of school refusal.

School refusal and other attendance problems

Until the 1930s, the different forms of persistent absence from school were all labelled truancy. In 1932 Broadwin identified a form of truancy characterized by neuroticism. The features included worry about the safety of mum, fear of the teacher, nervousness and running back home from school. A decade later Johnson *et al.* (1941) noted that 'there is a type of emotional disturbance in children, associated with great anxiety, that leads to serious absence from school' (p. 702). They referred to this phenomenon as school phobia. The term school refusal is preferred by many authors because it is more comprehensive than the term school phobia; it does not imply that the attendance problem is inevitably associated with specific stimuli located within the school setting (King *et al.*, 1996). For example, it may be associated with anxiety about separation from parents.

School refusal differs from truancy in a number of important ways:

➢ Truancy customarily entails an attempt to conceal non-attendance from the family (Berg, 1996). Truants may start out for school in the morning, but fail to arrive there or absent themselves during the day. Generally, truants will avoid going home. On the other hand, the school refuser's parents are well aware of the problem and the child often remains at home (Gordon and Young, 1976).

➢ Whereas the truant's non-attendance is usually intermittent, the school refuser may be away from school for weeks or months at a time (Gordon and Young, 1976).

➢ The school refuser is generally a good student with vocational goals requiring schooling, while the truant is usually an indifferent or poor student who dislikes school (Gordon and Young, 1976).

➢ Truancy often involves antisocial behaviour and truants are more often diagnosed with conduct disorder than with an emotional disorder (Hersov, 1985). Compared with school refusal, truancy is less often associated with anxiety symptoms (Berg *et al.*, 1993). Conversely, school refusers seldom display antisocial behaviour. Rather, they exhibit 'unwarranted fear' and display behaviours associated with the fear (Ollendick and King, 1990). Such behaviours may include refusing to get out of bed on school mornings, refusing to get dressed in school uniform, refusing to get in or out of the car during travel to school and clinging to parents. The avoidance of school attendance, whether in the form of reluctance or resistance and whether resulting in partial or total absence, is the essential feature.

Certainly, many children will exhibit occasional fear or anxiety in relation to school attendance, and as such it may be regarded as normal. However, this is very different to school refusal, which is a more serious matter. The essential features of school refusal are encompassed in a set of criteria which were originally developed by Berg *et al.* (1969) and which include refinements proposed by Bools *et al.* (1990) and Berg (1996):

> ➤ severe difficulty in attending school, often amounting to prolonged absence;
> ➤ when faced with the prospect of going to school with reasonable parental pressure, either severe emotional upset, shown by such symptoms as excessive fearfulness, undue temper and misery, or complaints of physical illness which do not have an obvious physical cause and which are thought to have an emotional basis;
> ➤ at some stage in the course of the attendance problem, the student stays at home with the knowledge of the parents when the school refuser should be at school.
> ➤ absence of conduct disorder (although some school refusers display aggressive and resistive behaviour this is usually confined to the home).

By specifying that there is reasonable parental pressure for the child to attend school, this definition encourages a distinction between school refusal and condoned absence, the latter being associated with parental irresponsibility in encouraging attendance. This alternative form of school attendance problem has been referred to as school withdrawal.

Determining what constitutes a case of school refusal can be difficult (Bools *et al.*, 1990). For example, long-standing school refusal may be mistaken for school withdrawal; that is, parents may appear not to be interested in their child's attendance, when in fact they have given up, unwillingly, their failing attempts to get their child to attend school.

Aetiology of school refusal

There is no single aetiology of school refusal; rather, the aetiology varies from child to child (Ollendick and Mayer, 1984). A broad range of precipitating factors associated with the home, the school and the individual may contribute to the development of school refusal. Commonly cited precipitating factors include:

> ➤ the transition from primary school to secondary school;
> ➤ illness in a family member;
> ➤ other family stresses such as moving home or parental separation;
> ➤ fear of some aspect of the school environment such as doing tests, social rejection or isolation, or having to use the school toilets.

Less commonly reported but equally important is the child's perception of his/her ability to cope with school (Heyne *et al.*, 1998). For example, students unsure of their capacity to fulfil academic requirements or to establish close friendships may be prone to avoid school.

The factors that serve to maintain the problem may be different from the initial precipitating factors. For example, a child who has been away from school for some time may come to fear being asked questions about the absence from school. The secondary gain associated with absence from school, including having access to the television, computer, toys, pets and many other benefits of life at home, may also serve to strengthen the refusal to attend school.

Confounding factors include the child's vulnerability as a consequence of biological or environmental factors. For example, the temperament of some children may predispose them to the development of anxiety problems (Rapee *et al.*, 2000). The family context can also be consequential. The parents of school refusers sometimes experience considerable anxiety or depression, or they experience couples distress, which can contribute to the children's stress and increase their vulnerability to negative experiences at school.

Learning theories have been employed both independently and inter-actively to account for the development and maintenance of school refusal. In sum, however, the aetiology of school refusal remains incompletely understood (King and Ollendick, 1989). At the clinical level, the best understanding of the factors contributing to an individual child's school refusal is gained by conducting a thorough assessment with the parents, the child and significant others, such as teachers, using a multi-method, multi-source problem-solving approach (cf. Ollendick and King, 1998).

Epidemiology of school refusal

Most commonly, school refusal is reported to affect about 1 per cent of the school-aged population (Burke and Silverman, 1987; Last and Strauss, 1990). Summarizing the rates reported for clinic-referred children, Hersov (1985) and Burke and Silverman (1987) suggested that the prevalence is approx-imately 5 per cent. Onset may be acute or chronic. For some school refusers non-attendance may be sporadic while others may have been absent from school for weeks or months. School refusal is equally common in boys and girls and occurs across the age range, with some suggestion of a higher prevalence in preadolescence and adolescence. There is a normal distribution of intelligence and no clear evidence that learning disabilities are over-represented in the general school refusal population. Socio-economic level and family composition do not appear to be associated with the incidence of school refusal.

Part I: Assessment

Having determined that the attendance problem is one of school refusal, as opposed to truancy or school withdrawal, the practitioner's task is to gather information that will help to plan effectively for intervention. Given the complex aetiology and varied presentation of school refusal, a thorough assessment is necessary to gain as complete an understanding of the problem as possible. We recommend a multi-method, multi-source (child, parents, school) approach to assessment, incorporating clinical interviews, diagnostic interviews, self-report measures and caregiver-completed measures.

At the School Refusal Clinic, the assessment with the family is conducted in two 1.5-hour sessions approximately one week apart. A dual practitioner model is employed, whereby one practitioner works with the young person and another works with the parents. At the start of the first assessment session, the two practitioners meet briefly with the child and parents together. The joint part of the session generally includes:

➢ friendly conversation aimed at 'breaking the ice';
➢ introduction to the practitioners, the clinic and its role;
➢ reinforcement of the family's decision to seek help;
➢ outline of the assessment process (e.g. 'We want to understand what has been happening in your situation, and we want to hear from everyone – child, parents and school – because everyone's view and experience is important');
➢ explanation of the procedure for the first session (e.g. parents and child are seen separately; clarify who will be working with whom, and where; assessment will involve answering questions, talking, filling in forms, playing games, and so on);
➢ discussion of limits to confidentiality;
➢ invitation to the parents and child to discuss briefly how they feel about coming to the clinic and what they hope might be achieved.

The issue of confidentiality can be difficult when operating under a dual practitioner model. We suggest to families that it is ideal if information can be shared freely between all parties involved (i.e. practitioners, child, parents, school). However, if there is information that a party would like to keep confidential (e.g. the child does not want the parents to know something or vice versa, or the child or parents do not want the school to know) then the practitioners will, of course, respect that. The client simply needs to indicate which information is 'off limits' for sharing. There are also the usual limits to confidentiality regarding harm to self or others. Almost without exception, families we have been involved with have been very happy to work with these provisions for confidentiality. This open sharing of information is often a key to implementing an effective, collaborative intervention.

After the initial joint session, the rest of the assessment is conducted with the child and parents separately. While gathering detailed information, the practitioner is also concerned to build rapport with the child or parents. The practitioner must be sensitive to factors such as the client's level of anxiety, interest and attention. For example, in order to maintain a child's attention, the practitioner might divide the 90-minute session as follows: 30 minutes of clinical interview, 20 minutes completing self-report questionnaires, 30 minutes of diagnostic interview, and 10 minutes of games or drawing. When working with non-responsive or highly anxious adolescents, the practitioner might choose to spend more time establishing rapport or to offer them the chance to focus on some questionnaires until they feel more like talking. Such flexibility is vital to establishing a therapeutic relationship and is important in setting the tone for intervention.

Clinical interview

Information from the clinical interview is used to obtain a well rounded picture of the child and his/her environment, to formulate hypotheses about specific school refusal behaviours and their controlling variables, and to select additional assessment methods to explore the school refusal problem further. The child and parents will often have different perspectives on the school refusal problem, and conducting separate interviews with them allows each the opportunity to freely discuss their views.

Child interview

School refusers frequently present as timid, shy, fearful and anxious, and they may be relatively unresponsive in the interview (King *et al.*, 1995). Therefore, it is important that the practitioner helps the child to feel at ease. Children should feel that they are positively regarded, accepted and respected by the practitioner regardless of behaviour. They should also feel that the practitioner is not there to give them the 'third degree' about school. As a result, it is usually wise to avoid raising the issue of school attendance early in the interview. Instead, the practitioner should demonstrate an interest in other aspects of the child's life by asking questions about pets, hobbies, family and friends. At our clinic, particularly with very anxious children, we would sometimes begin the session by playing a board game, gradually engaging the child in conversation through the course of the game.

Questions should be phrased in direct terms that the child will understand and it is important to provide support and encouragement when the child responds. Open-ended questions such as 'How do you feel about school?' or 'How are things going at school?' generally result in unelaborated responses such as, 'I don't know' or 'Okay'. The child can respond more easily and readily to specific questions such as 'What was it that first made you not want to go to school?' and 'What do your parents usually do when you tell them you are sick and don't want to go to school?' (King *et al.*, 1995).

A suggested schedule for the child clinical interview is included in Appendix 1. The interview tends to flow well in the sequence presented but the practitioner should also be flexible and follow the child's lead through the interview.

Parent interview

Questions to be explored are presented in the parent clinical interview schedule (Appendix 2). These questions cover issues such as:

➤ onset, duration and severity of the school refusal;
➤ precipitating factors;
➤ previous episodes of school refusal (including how these were overcome);
➤ associated symptoms (e.g. anxiety, somatic complaints, depression);
➤ a step-by-step account of the typical morning scenario (e.g. who is at home, what time the child gets out of bed; how the child expresses refusal to attend school);
➤ consequences for the school refusal behaviour, including activities that the child engages in when absent from school;
➤ perceptions of school life held by the child and parents;
➤ the child's academic performance;
➤ the child's social functioning.

Often the parents of school refusers present as anxious themselves. For this reason, we have found that it can be helpful to devote the entire first assessment session with the parents to the clinical interview before moving on to the other forms of assessment. This provides an extended opportunity for the parents to tell their 'story' and to share their distress in detail with the practitioner, an important aspect of building a therapeutic relationship with them. By the time of the second assessment session, the parents are often better able to focus on more specific assessment questions.

Blagg (1987, pp. 126–127) similarly emphasizes the need for the practitioner to be mindful of reducing parents' anxiety surrounding the school refusal problem. In particular, Blagg recommends that practitioners attend to the following points:

> ➤ Communicate a relaxed and unhurried manner to the clients.
> ➤ Thoroughly explore all the issues raised, paying attention to detail.
> ➤ Seek clarification when necessary.
> ➤ Help the parents to interpret the child's problems as transitory and understandable from a normal developmental perspective.
> ➤ Assist the parents in rationalizing guilt feelings by exploring reasonable explanations for the child's problems that do not necessarily involve the parents.

School interview

The assessment should not be limited to the child and parents; it is helpful to interview relevant staff at the child's school. This interview should be aimed at obtaining information about the child's social, emotional, behavioural and academic functioning at school, with a particular focus on any manifestation of anxious symptoms. Additionally, the interview provides an opportunity to start to build a working relationship with the school staff in preparation for the intervention phase. Finally, examination of the school attendance record may provide useful information about the extent and pattern of the child's non-attendance (e.g. avoidance of a particular day, subject or teacher).

Diagnostic interview

Whenever possible, clinical interviews should be supplemented with one of the more structured diagnostic interviews. In our work with school refusers we have found the Anxiety Disorders Interview Schedule for Children (ADIS; Silverman and Albano, 1996) to be very useful. The ADIS includes a Child Interview Schedule and a Parent Interview Schedule. The interviews are organized around diagnostic categories and permit differential diagnosis among major disorders from the perspective of both the child and the parent.

The ADIS is the only diagnostic interview designed specifically for anxiety-related disorders in children and adolescents, and as such it is a helpful tool in clarifying the nature and severity of anxiety problems associated with the child's school refusal. It is also extensive in its coverage, incorporating anxiety disorders, mood disorders and behaviour disorders. Use of the ADIS there-fore ensures that the breadth of possible problems associated with the child's school refusal is assessed.

Self-report measures

Self-report measures are an efficient means of assessing the young person's subjective experiences associated with school refusal. Such measures can draw our attention to specific symptoms experienced by the child and provide information about the severity of such symptoms using normative data. They can also be valuable in evaluating the effectiveness of an intervention by measuring changes in symptoms. In our assessment of school refusers, we routinely employ the following measures.

Fear Thermometer

The Fear Thermometer is a 0–100-point visual analogue scale on which children provide a rating of their emotional distress associated with school attendance (Appendix 3). Children rate how scared they were about going to school on the worst day in the past two weeks (0 = not scared, 100 = very scared). Once they have marked their response on the Fear Thermometer, the practitioner can follow up with questions about what happened on that day. The children's answers may shed light on situations that provoke the school refusal. A more immediate assessment of the level of fear is obtained by asking children to rate how scared they would be about going to school tomorrow. Again, the practitioner can take the opportunity to explore factors that might be associated with the anticipatory fear. Researchers have reported high reliability and acceptable validity for the Fear Thermometer and its variants in the assessment of child anxiety (Kleinknecht and Bernstein, 1988).

Fear Survey Schedule for Children – II

The Fear Survey Schedule for Children – II (FSSC-II; Gullone and King, 1992) is a recent adaptation of the Fear Survey Schedule for Children – Revised. The FSSC-II is a 75-item instrument designed to identify the prevalence and severity of fears in children and adolescents. Total fear scores can be derived from the overall scale as well as for each of the five factor subscales (Fear of Death and Danger, Fear of the Unknown, Fear of Failure and Criticism, Animal Fears, and Psychic Stress – Medical Fears). Reliability and validity have been established for this instrument (Gullone and King, 1992).

Revised Children's Manifest Anxiety Scale

The Revised Children's Manifest Anxiety Scale (R-CMAS; Reynolds and Richmond, 1978) is a 37-item instrument that assesses pervasive, non-situational anxiety. Representative anxiety items include 'I have trouble making up my mind', 'It is hard for me to keep my mind on my schoolwork', and

'Often I feel sick in the stomach'. Children respond to each of the items in a yes/no format. The scale yields three anxiety factors: Physiological Anxiety, Worry/Oversensitivity, and Social Concerns/Concentration. These can be useful in determining targets for intervention. For example, a school refuser who reports high levels of physiological anxiety may benefit from a focus on relaxation training. The R-CMAS has strong empirical support in terms of normative data, reliability and validity (Reynolds and Paget, 1983).

Children's Depression Inventory

As depression is often observed in school refusers, it can be useful to administer an instrument for measuring depressive symptoms. Among the most frequently used and psychometrically sound measures is the Children's Depression Inventory (CDI; Kovacs, 1981). The CDI consists of 27 items designed to assess a variety of symptoms of depression such as sleep disturbance, appetite loss, suicidal thoughts and general dysphoria. It also contains items addressing functioning at school. Each item consists of three statements that reflect normal responses, moderate depressive symptoms or severe depressive symptoms. Children choose the statement that best describes them (for example, for item 15, the statements are 'Doing schoolwork is not a big problem', 'I have to push myself many times to do my schoolwork' and 'I have to push myself all the time to do my schoolwork').

Self-Efficacy Questionnaire for School Situations

The Self-Efficacy Questionnaire for School Situations (SEQ-SS; Heyne *et al.*, 1998) was developed to assess children's perceived ability to cope with specific anxiety-provoking situations associated with school attendance. The instrument encompasses 12 situations (e.g. being teased or bullied at school; separation from mother and father) and each is rated on a five-point scale from 1 = 'Definitely couldn't cope' to 5 = 'Definitely could cope'. It yields a total self-efficacy score along with subscale scores for Academic/Social Stress and Separation/Discipline Stress. Psychometric evaluation suggests that the SEQ-SS has promising validity and reliability (Heyne *et al.*, 1998).

Self-Statements Assessment

Some authors (e.g. Rapee *et al.*, 2000) have suggested that irrational or dysfunctional cognitions may play a role in the development of anxiety and school refusal. At the School Refusal Clinic, we developed a verbally administered questionnaire designed to tap into some of the child's cognitions that may be contributing to anxiety and school refusal. The Self-Statements Assessment aims to elicit the child's thoughts about seven aspects of school attendance:

➢ going to school;
➢ separation from parents;
➢ schoolwork;
➢ teachers
➢ the head teacher;
➢ other children at school.

In addition to these specific factors, the child is given the opportunity to nominate any other reasons for the reluctance to attend school.

The practitioner introduces the Self-Statements Assessment to the child in the following way:

> Have you ever played a game where someone says a word and you have to say the first thing that comes into your head? For instance, if I said 'chocolate', what is the first thought that comes into your head?

The practitioner reinforces the child's response, keeping a light manner that emphasizes the fun, game-like nature of the task. If the child seems not to understand the instruction, the practitioner can model verbalizing his/her own thoughts about the item. The next step involves asking the child to report thoughts regarding a situation (e.g. going to the beach; playing basketball; Christmas). Again, when necessary, the practitioner can model a response, such as 'My thoughts about going to the beach are having the sun on my face, playing in the sand, and feeling relaxed and happy'.

Once the child demonstrates an ability to verbalize thoughts through these practice items, the practitioner begins the assessment of self-statements about the school-related items. The practitioner moves through the items in a sequential manner, prefacing each item with the request 'Tell me what thoughts you have about...'. After the child's initial response, the practitioner waits five seconds and then asks the child, 'Any other thoughts?' Many children will further elaborate on their cognitions when probed in this way. For each item, the process continues until the child indicates that she/he does not have any other thoughts. The child's self-statements are recorded verbatim, either by audio/video recording or transcribed by the practitioner. The information obtained may be useful in defining the nature of the school refusal problem and in guiding the intervention by highlighting specific areas and cognitions to target.

Functional analysis

Given the multiple causes of school refusal, practitioners and researchers recommend that functional analysis be a key aspect of the assessment process (e.g. King *et al.*, 1995; Kearney and Albano, 2000). One instrument providing a functional analysis of school refusal is the School Refusal Assessment Scale (SRAS), developed by Kearney and Silverman (1993). It is a 16-item instrument designed to identify maintaining variables associated with school refusal. Specifically, the SRAS assesses four factors which may maintain school refusal:

➢ avoidance of stimuli which provoke specific fearfulness or general anxiousness (function 1);
➢ escape from aversive social or evaluative situations (function 2);
➢ attention-getting behaviours which reflect separation concerns (function 3);
➢ behaviours which gain positive tangible reinforcement (function 4).

The category includes children who are fearful of some specific stimulus in the school setting, such as being in a particular room. The second category includes those who are socially anxious and who are apprehensive about evaluative situations at school (e.g. speaking in front of the class). The third category includes those who engage in attention-getting behaviour such as tantrums or complaining of illness in an effort to be allowed to stay home. Those in the fourth category remain home in order to engage in enjoyable activities such as going out and seeing other people during the day.

Each question is rated on a Likert-type scale from 0 to 6 (from *never* to *always*). Item means for the four functional categories are calculated and compared with each other. The highest-scoring condition is considered to be the primary factor maintaining the school refusal.

Kearney and Albano (2000) also provide prescriptive guidelines for treatment based on the results of the SRAS. For instance, relaxation training and desensitization might be indicated for children who score highest on function 1; social skills training would be appropriate for those who score highest on function 2; shaping and reinforcement would be used with children who score highest on function 3; and contingency management is suggested for those who score highest on function 4. The information derived from the SRAS is ideally combined with other assessment information in the development of a comprehensive intervention plan.

Separate forms of the SRAS have been developed for use with the child, parents and teachers. Kearney and Silverman (1993) report that the SRAS has good test–retest reliability and to have concurrent validity with other instruments, including the Anxiety Disorders Interview Schedule for Children.

Caregiver-completed measures

Child Behavior Checklist

Parents' ratings of the child's social competency and behaviour problems can be obtained using the Child Behavior Checklist (CBCL; Achenbach, 1991a).

Each of the behaviour problem items is scored using a 0–2 scale (0 = not true; 1 = somewhat true; 2 = often true). The CBCL yields a Total Behavior Problems score and scores for two broadband dimensions – Internalizing and Externalizing. It also has a number of symptom subscales: Withdrawn, Somatic, Anxious/Depressed, Social Problems, Thought Problems, Attention Problems, Aggressive Behavior, and Delinquent Behavior. The internalizing scales are particularly relevant in the assessment of school refusal but useful information can be gained from the externalizing scales as well. The CBCL has extensive normative data that aid in the assessment of the level of functional impairment for the child. The CBCL is a widely used and well respected clinical research instrument with established reliability and validity (Daugherty and Shapiro, 1994).

Self-Statements Assessment

The Self-Statements Assessment – Parent Form is designed to elicit parents' cognitions about why their child is refusing to attend school, how the problem ought to be addressed and their role in managing their child's behaviour. In dual-parent families, emphasis is placed upon both parents responding to this verbally administered questionnaire, given that their perspectives and opinions are sometimes quite different. The information gathered is valuable in directing intervention, particularly as it highlights the potential importance of conducting cognitive therapy with the parents.

The practitioner will usually begin with the following introduction to the instrument to parents:

> It is often helpful to hear parents' thoughts about what school refusal is, and how it can be addressed. So I'd like to hear what thoughts you (each) have about these things. Even if you haven't thought a lot about these things before, I'd be interested to hear what comes to mind for you just now as you think about it. If it's okay with you, while you talk, I'll jot down your responses. Tell me what thoughts you currently have about…

The instrument consists of the following questions:

➤ why the child does not attend school regularly and voluntarily;
➤ how important it is for parents to be involved in dealing with a child who has school attendance difficulties;
➤ what things the parents can do to help the child with school attendance difficulties;
➤ who ought to be most responsible for the child's attendance at school;
➤ how the child would cope with regular school attendance;
➤ how quickly a child ought to return to school after having been absent due to school refusal;

➤ the fact that when the child is at school he/she is separated from the parents.

Teacher's Report Form

The Teacher's Report Form (TRF; Achenbach, 1991b) provides a rating by the child's teacher or school counsellor of the child's adaptive functioning and problem behaviours in the school setting. The information obtained on the TRF can be compared and contrasted with the parents' reports on the CBCL, in order to develop a full understanding of the child's behaviour across settings. Like the CBCL, the psychometric properties of the TRF have considerable research support (Daugherty and Shapiro, 1994).

Communicating assessment findings

Having obtained much information during the assessment, the practitioners meet together to develop a composite diagnosis and arrive at a shared case formulation. Information from clinical interviews with the child, parent and school, questionnaire data and diagnostic information should all be taken into account when preparing such a formulation.

In our work with school refusers and their families, we prepare a written summary of the information obtained during the assessment, which includes each person's view of the school refusal problem, questionnaire results, diagnostic information and formulation. We then conduct a 'feedback session' with the child and parents, usually separately, in which we explain the findings of the assessment and relate this to plans for intervention. Throughout the feedback session the child or parents are invited to comment on, clarify or question the information discussed. By regularly consulting with the child and parents about the findings, we aim to develop a shared understanding of the problem and to foster a collaborative approach to intervention. Relevant school staff are also contacted and briefed on the assessment findings.

Part II: General considerations for intervention

The intervention model consists of approximately eight one-hour sessions with the parents and eight one-hour sessions with the child. The sessions are generally conducted twice-weekly over four weeks, and they are individual sessions (as opposed to group therapy). School return is scheduled about halfway through the intervention, following skills acquisition, and allowing for trouble-shooting after the planned return. Consultation with school personnel occurs during a school visit scheduled before the child's school return and via regular telephone contact after. Of course, variations are likely to occur in accordance with the severity of the school refusal problem, the time taken to develop a trusting, working relationship with the parents and child, school and family holidays, and illness or other unforeseen factors.

Child sessions are predicated upon school refusers acquiring and employing strategies for managing their anxiety, in order to make school return and regular attendance more achievable. Parent sessions are based upon the role that parents can play in managing the environmental contingencies that are maintaining the school refusal and those that lead to the development of school attendance. School staff play an important role in managing the contingencies specific to the school environment.

The child-, parent- and school-based interventions presented involve the judicious selection of specific intervention components. This individualized approach rests upon the complex array of aetiological and maintenance factors, together with the need to be sensitive to the individuality of each child, family and school situation. In particular, child factors include developmental level and diagnostic profile, the function of the school refusal as determined by the SRAS (see above), the history and severity of school refusal, and variations in cognitive, physiological and behavioural response systems.

Often, parents and school staff have made a number of efforts to return the child to regular attendance, with limited or no success. By presenting the current intervention as an integrated approach between child, parents, school staff and practitioner, therapeutic leverage may be gained, and parents and school staff may be helped to engage in the current approach. While some of the strategies may be similar or identical to those previously employed, the difference emerges in the integration of a range of strategies.

When working with families in which there are two parents, it is almost always imperative that both the father and mother be involved in the intervention. This may take some persistent encouragement (and flexibility in scheduling appointments) on behalf of the practitioner. Only when both parents are involved in the intervention process can the practitioner adequately address fundamental issues such as parents developing a united approach to managing the problem, parents supporting each other during the stressful process of school return, and taking advantage of the greater influence that one parent may have over the behaviour of the young person. While single parents lack partner support in managing the problem, unpublished data suggest that the outcomes for children from single-parent families are not inferior (Heyne, 1999). Often a major challenge for single parents is in finding alternative sources of assistance for the process of escorting the child to school.

A dual practitioner model is employed from the start of assessment and throughout intervention, whereby one practitioner works with the child while another works with the parents. As well as having practical advantages (e.g. reducing the need for families to make twice as many visits to the clinic to see the one practitioner, or for family members to have to wait for extended periods in the waiting room while the practitioner meets with both parties successively), it serves two important therapeutic functions. First, it affords the practitioner working with the child a greater opportunity to establish a therapeutic relationship. Rather than seeing the practitioner as aligned with the parents, the child may perceive a greater alignment between him/herself and the practitioner, which facilitates openness and collaboration. Second, families benefit from the knowledge, expertise and the ideas of two practitioners, and practitioners have the opportunity to consult with each other.

Occasionally, joint sessions are held with the parents and child. Joint sessions may be used, for example, to facilitate problem solving between parents and adolescent school refusers regarding the decision about school placement (see 'Preliminary considerations', below). The parents and child may come together to negotiate a contract for positive reinforcement (see 'Positive reinforcement', below). Some joint time may be scheduled towards the end of some sessions in order to review the strategies being covered. For those cases where parents are highly critical of the child's progress, practitioners may choose to refrain from bringing the parents and child together at the beginning of a session following a scheduled school return. This prevents the child being exposed to the parents' criticisms and, instead, gives the practitioner an opportunity to tease out and reinforce any small achievements the child may have made.

Early implementation of the intervention programme is prudent. The longer the children are away from school, the harder it becomes for them to return. Anxiety may grow with regard to keeping up with schoolwork, fitting in with friends and explaining absences. In addition, the advantages associated with not being at school may strengthen the avoidance of school return.

In working with children, parents and school personnel, a strong emphasis is placed upon being well prepared for the child's school return. The child is well equipped with coping strategies, parents are led to consider their responses to a range of possible scenarios on the day of the child's return, and school staff need to make arrangements for the child's smooth transition back into the school setting. While being careful not to cultivate anxiety about possible problems, the practitioner can predict possible 'hiccups' in order to reduce the chance that parents will be overcome with anxiety or anger in the face of such events.

The intervention programme outlined below is applicable to school refusers whose attendance is non-existent or sporadic, and those who attend school regularly but who display excessive reluctance to attend. It has been written with the worst-case scenario in mind (i.e. complete non-attendance). When a child is attending regularly but under duress, the practitioner may need to make some modifications. Time would not need to be spent on negotiating a date and plan for school return, but greater consideration might need to be given to:

➢ the identification of ongoing stressors or parental responses which may be maintaining the child's fear or anxiety;
➢ the implementation of desensitization hierarchies not directly related to school attendance, such as social involvement outside school hours, or separation from parents outside school hours;
➢ extra support for the child within the school setting;
➢ greater attention to the child's anxiety-producing self-talk;
➢ increased support and encouragement for parents who may be inclined to abandon their efforts prematurely.

The intervention also needs to be modified according to the developmental level of the school refuser. For example, cognitive strategies with the younger child are more concrete in nature. The decision about school placement and the type of school return (immediate versus graded) involves greater discussion between parents and adolescent refusers. At the school level, the scope and nature of positive reinforcement varies between primary and secondary schooling levels, and more attention needs to be paid to the impact of academic pressures upon secondary students. (For further discussion of the impact of the child's developmental level on the application of cognitive-behavioural interventions, see Holmbeck *et al.*, 2000).

Part III: Intervention with the young person

Child treatment involves the use of behavioural and cognitive procedures directly with the young person. This level of intervention aims to help the child cope with the stressors associated with returning to school or maintaining regular school attendance (e.g. bullying by peers; separation from parents). The four major components of child treatment are:

> relaxation training;
> cognitive therapy;
> enhancement of social competence;
> exposure.

These components should be applied flexibly, depending on the child's diagnostic profile, the function of the school refusal and the child's developmental level.

Relaxation training

For those young people with strong physiological manifestations of anxiety (e.g. nausea, rapid breathing, 'butterflies' in the stomach), as may be indicated on the R-CMAS or in the diagnostic information, relaxation can be a helpful coping skill. It aims to provide the child with a means of combating physiological discomfort in stressful situations at home and school (e.g. preparing for school on the day of return; approaching the school grounds; being asked questions by peers). Helping children to recognize unwanted anxious arousal and, more importantly, to prevent or reduce discomforting feelings places them in a better position to employ the full range of coping strategies they learn.

One of the most commonly used methods of relaxation training is progressive muscle relaxation. Two useful training scripts are those by Koeppen (1974) for younger children and Ollendick and Cerny (1981) for older children and adolescents. These authors recommend 15-minute training sessions, with no more than three muscle groups being introduced in any one session of training. The in-session training is ideally complemented by practice at home using a tape-recording of a training session. Cue-controlled relaxation training can be achieved by having the children control their breathing rate and sub-vocalizing the word 'relax' as they exhale, at numerous points throughout the progressive muscle relaxation training. In this way, with sufficient practice, the child can induce full body relaxation. Throughout relaxation training, the practitioner and child should discuss the best places and times to practise relaxation and what the applications of the skill might be.

Some children will enjoy supplementing progressive muscle relaxation training with guided imagery. Using this method, children picture themselves feeling very calm and relaxed in a favourite setting, real or imagined. The practitioner guides children's imagery by providing scene-related prompts. (See Rapee *et al.*, 2000, for examples of standardized scenes.)

Some children will report that they do not feel any benefit from relaxation training, even after considerable practice. Others will fail to practise sufficiently at home. Often these children respond better to shorter forms of relaxation training (e.g. controlled breathing alone) or to a more active training process, such as the 'robot–rag doll' technique for younger children (Kendall *et al.*, 1992a). In this exercise, children are directed to walk around the room pretending that they are a robot, with body stiff and rigid. They then pretend they are a rag doll, with a loose and floppy body. The practitioner encourages children to notice the different sensations in their muscles (i.e. tense versus relaxed) and to identify situations in which it would be helpful to relax one's muscles 'like a rag doll'.

Cognitive therapy

In our experience, a vital aspect of intervention with school refusers is a focus on the child's cognitions. Anxious school refusers are likely to process information in a distorted manner and engage in maladaptive self-talk, perpetuating their anxiety. Typical cognitive distortions may include:

➢ *overestimation of the probability of unpleasant events occurring* (e.g. Mum will fall ill while I'm at school);
➢ *underestimation of one's ability to cope with unpleasant events* (e.g. I won't be able to give the talk in front of the class);
➢ *a perception of unpleasant events as catastrophic* (e.g. It's awful and unbearable when the teacher raises her voice);
➢ *negative self-evaluations* (e.g. I'm hopeless at sport);
➢ *interpretation of ambiguous information as threatening* (e.g. John did not ask me to his party – he hates me!).

The aim of cognitive therapy is to effect a change in the child's emotions and behaviour, to facilitate school attendance by modifying maladaptive cognitions.

The Seven Ds is a mnemonic device to aid practitioners in the process of conducting cognitive therapy:

➢ Describe;
➢ Detect;
➢ Determine;
➢ Dispute;
➢ Discover;
➢ Do;
➢ Discuss.

Although presented below in a seemingly logical sequence for doing cognitive therapy, in practice the process is a fluid one, with the practitioner moving back and forward between the various components as necessary.

1. Describe

The first step involves a description of the 'cognitive connection', the notion that how we feel and behave is affected by how we think. In working with children and adolescents, visual aides such as cartoons depicting different thoughts and emotions of characters, educational handouts and blackboard presentations can offer a useful supplement to the practitioner's explanation. For children, we have found Kendall's (1992) 'Cat and Dog' cartoon useful in this respect. Some useful educational materials for adolescents can be found in Clarke *et al.* (1990).

2. Detect

This process involves helping the child to identify thoughts and feelings associated with school attendance or other anxiety-provoking situations. Cartoons with empty thought bubbles can be useful (cf. Kendall *et al.*, 1992a). The practitioner can present a cartoon to the child and ask the child to identify what the characters in the cartoon might be thinking and feeling. Initially the cartoons might involve simple non-threatening situations but then cartoons depicting anxiety-eliciting situations can be introduced. Cartoons that depict school-related scenes are particularly relevant for school refusers.

Another useful exercise is verbally to present the child with scenarios and ask the child to nominate what the characters might be thinking. For example, 'Jane sees some girls whispering together. When they see Jane standing there, they laugh and run off. What might Jane be thinking?'

Once children understand the concept of identifying thoughts, the practitioner can work on helping them to become aware of their own self-talk. Questions such as the following may be useful in eliciting the child's cognitions:

> ➢ What would keep you from going to school tomorrow?
> ➢ What are your thoughts about going to school tomorrow?
> ➢ When you tried to go back to school today what thoughts were going through your head?
> ➢ What is the hardest thing for you about facing school again?
> ➢ What would it mean if you couldn't answer a question in class?
> ➢ What would be the worst thing about staying the whole day at school?

Often children will find it difficult to recognize their own thoughts and it may be necessary for the practitioner to provide some general prompts, such as 'Were you thinking about being away from mum? The schoolwork? Seeing the other students?' However, the practitioner should be careful not to pressure unduly those children who find it difficult to pinpoint why they cannot face school.

3. Determine

Once children have identified some cognitions, they can be asked to evaluate each thought to determine whether it is a helpful or unhelpful thought. Even young children are usually able to do this quite easily. Referring again to the 'cognitive connection', the practitioner can help children to understand the link between unhelpful thoughts and negative feelings, and between helpful thoughts and positive feelings.

4. Dispute

Having detected the child's thoughts and determined that there are some that are unhelpful or irrational and contributing to significant distress, the next step is to dispute these maladaptive cognitions. In this process, children are helped to challenge and debate with themselves about their irrational cognitions with a view to developing a more sensible or rational appraisal of the situation.

One of the most commonly used disputational techniques relies on the practitioner questioning in such a way that clients are forced critically to appraise the logic of some of their thoughts or beliefs (Bernard and Joyce, 1984). These questions challenge clients to provide evidence for their beliefs, to estimate (realistically) the probability of a negative outcome in a situation, to consider alternative ways of interpreting a situation, or to evaluate whether the cognition is helping them to achieve their goals. In working with school refusers this may translate into questions such as:

> ➢ Where is the evidence that you cannot cope with school? When have you coped at school before?

> ➤ How likely is it that the teacher will yell at you?
> ➤ How awful would it be it to miss your mother when you are at school?
> ➤ Is it sensible to say you hate school when there are parts of school you really like?
> ➤ Will thinking this way help you to get your life back on track, doing what other 14-year-olds are doing?

5. Discover

Following on from disputation, the child is helped to discover and employ alternative, adaptive self-statements about anxiety-provoking situations. Sometimes referred to as 'coping statements', these are tools for the child to use in coping with feared situations. Some children find it very difficult to generate their own coping statements. We have found that some respond well to selecting from a list of pre-prepared coping statements, or hearing about statements used by other school refusers. Below are some examples of coping statements for dealing with situations commonly problematic for school refusers:

Situation	Coping statement
Having to go to school	Every day I'm there it will get easier. I can cope with being at school. Just do it!
Having to take the next step in an attendance plan	I can do it. I stuck to my plan today – I can do it again tomorrow.
Experiencing physiological arousal	This is just anxiety. I know how to manage these feelings.
Being away from mother	Mum will be all right while I'm at school. I'll see her at the end of the day.
Answering questions about absence	Not everyone will ask me questions and, if they do, I know what to say.
Having to give a talk to the class	Everyone gets a bit nervous before giving a talk. If others can see I'm nervous, so what?
Being teased or bullied	I'm an okay kid. I don't have to believe what that person says about me.

6. Do

'Do' is a prompt for the practitioner to set an appropriate between-session practice task in relation to cognitive therapy. This might include exercises such as self-monitoring thoughts; developing additional coping statements; polling family and friends regarding the accuracy or helpfulness of a particular cognition; or doing a behavioural experiment. Behavioural experiments can be a very powerful way of helping children to change their thinking. For example, one young boy was set the task of asking to join in with peers at school in order to test his assumption that he would be rejected. Another young person was encouraged to take up her teacher's offer to provide extra help with mathematics to challenge her belief that 'teachers don't care about me'.

Children can also be challenged to find ways of remembering to use their new, more helpful ways of thinking. For instance, some children write their coping statements on a card to carry with them and refer to as necessary. One young boy we worked with included the affirmation 'Don't worry, be happy' as part of his armoury of coping statements. He then symbolized this statement with a 'smiley face' and drew it on his hand, pencil case and schoolbooks. Whenever he felt anxious about being away from his mother during the school day, he would look at one of the smiley faces and remember his coping statement.

7. Discuss

Discuss is a prompt for the practitioner to review the practice task at the following session and to praise or reward children for their efforts or achievements in attempting the task. If the child has forgotten or neglected to do a practice task, some time can be allocated in session to complete it. This emphasizes to the child that practice tasks are an important part of the intervention. Discussion around ways to remember to do practice tasks may also be necessary with some children. Information derived from completion of the practice task provides a good springboard for further cognitive therapy work in-session. The practitioner may continue the cognitive therapy by setting a new challenge or task that builds on the child's previous practice task(s).

Age-appropriate techniques

Several authors (e.g. Bernard and Joyce, 1984) point to the need for practitioners to consider developmental factors when selecting cognitive therapy techniques for children. For instance, Piagetian theory informs us that younger children will have difficulty with abstract thinking and seeing the perspective of others. Thus, in working with younger children, the practitioner will need to present cognitive therapy concepts in a concrete way, using lots of teaching examples. Use of pictures, cartoons or a blackboard or whiteboard can not only facilitate greater understanding of the concepts presented but may also serve to engage the child in the treatment process. In their guidelines for the selection of age-appropriate cognitive techniques, Bernard and Joyce (1984) suggest that the practitioner rely on instruction in rational self-statements (akin to the 'discover' step) for children less than seven years and incorporate disputation of irrational beliefs (the 'dispute' step) for children who are 11 years and older.

Problem-solving

Problem-solving often complements cognitive therapy, particularly when a child or adolescent is 'stuck' on a particular problem or dilemma. Problem-solving training involves teaching the child a method for thinking about and solving the problem. Typically, the approach includes the following steps:

➢ defining the problem;
➢ identifying possible solutions;
➢ evaluating the positives and negatives of each proposal;
➢ selecting and implementing a solution;
➢ evaluating the outcome.

Encouraging children to self-reinforce their efforts or achievements can be an important adjunctive step. Once learned, children can be encouraged to draw on their problem-solving skills to address any problems that arise throughout the intervention and beyond.

One problem that commonly arises for school refusers is the issue of whether to change schools. Some young people become quite fixed on this as a solution to overcoming their school refusal. We have found a problem-solving approach to be helpful in encouraging the child or adolescent to think broadly about the advantages and disadvantages that may be associated with such a change. Below is a list of 'pros' and 'cons' developed by a 13-year-old school refuser:

	Pros	Cons
Return to same school	Teachers know me Have friends Might not have to repeat a grade	Don't like the teachers Teasing Don't like the other kids
	Pros	**Cons**
New school	Make new friends Different teachers	Teachers don't know me Cost Might be hard to make friends Might have to repeat Might not be happy there

Having carefully considered the advantages and disadvantages of moving to another school, many children will opt to return to the familiar surroundings of their current school. Others will become more resolved in their desire to change schools. Of course, it is necessary to involve the parents in discussion and decision-making around this issue.

Enhancement of social competence

There are two main indications for social skills training with school refusers. The first relates to social skills deficits, which may have contributed to the development of a school refusal problem. For instance, the child may lack strategies for dealing with teasing or bullying, or being socially isolated at school. Training the child in skills for joining in with peers, initiating friendships and dealing assertively with harassment can be most beneficial for these children. Children can be provided with short handouts on key aspects of these skills (e.g. 'Joining In'; 'Standing Up for Yourself'). We have found material from Spence (1995) and McGrath and Francey (1991) to be excellent for this purpose. The practitioner models the desired social behaviours and then the child rehearses the behaviours through role-plays, receiving reinforcing and corrective feedback from the practitioner.

The second area in which social skills training can be important relates to the social anxiety that many school refusers experience with respect to answering peers' or teachers' questions about their absence. Regardless of what precipitated the school refusal, concerns about being able to face peers upon returning to school often become paramount for the school refuser, as indicated in the SEQ-SS. This is particularly so for children who have been absent from school for some time. The practitioner can help children to feel more confident in their ability to deal with questions regarding absence by following these steps:

> Brainstorm possible responses the child might give to questions such as 'Where have you been?' and 'Why were you away from school?' Encourage the child to consider common reasons why children are absent from school (e.g. illness, holiday) and allow children to be creative and to include untruths if they wish.

> Ask children to select a response they think might be reasonable to give.

> Role-play with children a situation at school where someone asks about their absence. Have children play the role of themselves, while the practitioner plays the role of a peer. Initially the practitioner should act as a kind, non-threatening peer who immediately accepts the child's proffered excuse and welcomes the child back to school.

➤ Ask children to reflect on the role-play, including comment on how comfortable they felt and whether the response worked well. The practitioner should provide feedback about how confident the children seemed and how well they handled the questions posed.

➤ The practitioner should then initiate another role-play, informing children that the practitioner will now play the role of a more curious and persistent peer. During the role-play the practitioner should aim to question the veracity of the explanation for the absence and perhaps even call the student some derogatory names.

➤ Again, ask children to rate their level of comfort and judge whether the response they gave held up under scrutiny. Usually through this process, children who have fabricated a reason for their absence will recognize the pitfalls inherent in this and will usually opt for an honest explanation (e.g. 'I didn't want to come to school'; 'I was at home').

➤ It can be helpful, too, to give children some ideas about how to end a conversation about absence from school assertively, such as saying 'Anyway, I'm back now. What's happening today?' or 'I don't really want to talk about that now'.

Skills practised during the session(s) are further developed through the use of practice tasks. These are usually aimed at encouraging children to increase their knowledge of social skills or to apply their social skills in real life. For instance, possible practice tasks could include observing how others initiate conversations, telephoning a friend or taking a ball to school and inviting other children to join a game.

Exposure

Of course, the aim of the intervention is for the child to return to school or, if attending sporadically, to increase the current level of attendance. In this way, exposure to the anxiety-provoking situation (i.e. attending school) is a crucial component in the treatment of school refusal.

Exposure can be imaginal or real life (otherwise known as *in vivo* exposure). Ultimately, for the child to attend school, *in vivo* exposure needs to occur. However, imaginal exposure may need to precede real-life exposure, particularly when the child experiences a very high level of anxiety. Systematic desensitization is a form of imaginal exposure involving three steps (King *et al.*, 1995):

➤ constructing a hierarchy of anxiety-evoking situations;
➤ teaching the child a relaxation skill;

➤ progressive imaginal exposure of the child to the hierarchy items while in a relaxed state.

Presented here is an example of an anxiety hierarchy developed with an 11-year-old school refuser and employed during imaginal systematic desensitization:

➤ touch school clothes;
➤ look at photographs of school;
➤ walk halfway to school;
➤ walk up to school;
➤ walk around the outside of the school;
➤ walk around the outside of the school in school uniform;
➤ walk around the school and inside the school gates;
➤ meet with the class teacher, with parents present;
➤ meet with the class teacher, without parents;
➤ attend empty class with teacher;
➤ attend regular class for first lesson;
➤ attend regular class until lunch;
➤ attend regular class for whole day.

Another form of imaginal exposure is emotive imagery, which is especially helpful in working with children of primary school age (King *et al.*, 1995). Instead of relaxation, the anxiety inhibitor is a series of exciting stories that evoke feelings of pride, confidence and happiness. Children are asked to close their eyes and imagine the events described in the story and to answer story-related questions asked by the practitioner. The stories might incorporate hero figures who attend school with the child, single the child out for special privileges and help the child to cope with challenging situations.

Emotive imagery was used with an 11-year-old boy who attended our clinic. He developed separation anxiety after his mother had an operation. This developed into school refusal as he worried about being at school and his mother falling ill. The child nominated a high-profile football player as his hero. Emotive imagery was incorporated in three treatment sessions before his return to school. An excerpt from the emotive imagery treatment follows:

Nathan Burke arrives at your home. He explains that he has heard you are returning to school today and he would like to come along with you. You are very excited at this news. Nathan drives you to school in his hot sports car and you sit next to him in the front seat. You feel strong and confident being with Nathan. Now you are at school. Lots of kids gather around the car to admire Nathan and to welcome you back to school. Nathan tells everyone that he is here to spend the day with you. You feel really proud that Nathan is with YOU and the other kids are so pleased that you have brought Nathan Burke to their school. They can hardly believe it! Everyone's laughing and cheering and patting you and Nathan on the back as you walk towards the classroom. At this point you think of your mother and wonder how she is at home.... [Further along the hierarchy] At lunch Nathan takes you down to the playing field to kick the football. All of the other kids join in. Everyone is having so much fun. You feel happy and relaxed. Nothing could wipe the smile off your face. This is a day at school you will never forget! You think of your mum and remember that she had been unwell.

Graded or immediate full return to school?

While imaginal exposure is often reported in the treatment of anxious or phobic children, for school refusers we tend to rely more heavily on real-life exposure. Sometimes this involves the child's return to immediate full-time schooling but more often the child's attendance is increased gradually. Immediate return to full-time schooling is usually tried with younger children and those who have not been absent from school for very long. The gradual approach is more commonly employed with adolescents, with children who have been absent from school for several weeks or months, or children with very high anxiety. When possible, the practitioner should involve the child in negotiations regarding the method for school return. This is particularly important when working with adolescents. Giving the child some control over the development of the process for school return can help to reduce the young person's resistance. Rather than the practitioner prescribing the approach to school return, the child is encouraged to evaluate the merits of an immediate full-time return versus a graded return. Some children may elect an immediate full-time return to reduce embarrassment about having to leave school earlier than other students. Others may consider that returning for just a few classes, or even as little as 15 minutes, would make the initial return to school easier.

When employing a graded approach to school return, a good starting point is to engage children in a discussion around the component steps of going to school (e.g. getting out of bed; eating breakfast; getting in the car; walking into the building; attending the first class; attending the second class and so on). They might then be asked to identify which of these steps they think they could achieve currently. For instance, they might feel confident that they could dress in school uniform, be driven to school and talk to their teacher (but not go to class). An 'attendance plan' might then be developed with this as a starting point.

Sometimes children want to aim for a level of attendance that the practitioner may regard as somewhat ambitious given the high level of anxiety experienced by the child or a long absence from school. Sensitive handling of this issue by the practitioner is required. It is important that the first step be achievable for the young person. An initial experience of success can build confidence and motivation to continue work through the attendance plan. So as not to undermine the child's expressed confidence, the practitioner can include the child's nominated goal (e.g. attending five out of six classes) in the attendance plan, while suggesting a minimum step to be achieved (e.g. attending at least until recess).

Children encouraged to adopt a 'stepladder' approach to the attendance plan such that each day they aim to achieve at least the same as the previous day, or else to move up a step on the plan (e.g. more time at school, or more time in the classroom). However, children should try to avoid going backwards. The following is an example of an initial attendance plan developed with a 12-year-old girl. She developed a fear of being in the classroom with her classmates and this led to school refusal. However, when her mother could get her to school, she would stay quite happily in the Student Welfare Centre (SWC), where the school counsellor was located.

Tuesday	Go to SWC until morning recess Attend classes 3 and 4 after recess After lunch, attend class or go to SWC
Wednesday	Go to SWC until morning recess Attend classes 3–5
Thursday	Go to SWC until morning recess Attend classes 3–6
Friday	Spend 1 hour in SWC Attend classes 2–6
Monday	Spend 1 hour in SWC Attend classes 2–6

The attendance plans often need to be revamped during the course of treatment. Some children will progress through the steps as planned but the majority will experience some setbacks. The scheduling of frequent appointments during this phase ensures that the practitioner can readily offer encouragement and support in reviewing the plan and help maintain the momentum in the child's efforts at attending school.

A reward contract can be used in conjunction with the attendance plan. Contracted rewards include those rewards able to be administered by the practitioner (e.g. extra time to play games or watch a favourite video together; sweets or cakes; a special tour of the clinical setting) or by the child's parents, as negotiated by the child. At our clinic, we have been repeatedly surprised by the motivating effect that even a simple in-session reward can have for a child. This seems to be particularly so when there is a high level of rapport between the practitioner and child.

Ultimately, any return to school constitutes exposure, whether achieved suddenly or gradually, or facilitated by imaginal or *in vivo* methods. A process of covert exposure even occurs through the practitioner engaging the child in regular, calm discussions about school. It is during the exposure phase that the practitioner usually needs to be particularly flexible, patiently setting and resetting the steps in the child's attendance plan until some progress occurs. Of course, any level of success is praiseworthy, even if the nominated step or goal is not fully achieved. A positive outlook on the child's progress, even if it is slow, is likely to be more effective in the long run.

Facilitating the process

In addition to the major treatment components outlined above, there are key process issues that support and guide the intervention with the young person.

The issue of school return should be gently but clearly introduced to the agenda of sessions, with the practitioner modelling confidence in the child's ability to learn how to cope with school return. The topic of school return can be discussed in the context of facing fears in order to overcome them, often in a stepwise fashion. Children can be encouraged to think about the similarities with other fear-related situations they have overcome in the past, or how a hero figure may overcome fears (cf. Blagg, 1987).

Discussion about the date for school return should be carefully timed. At the School Refusal Clinic this discussion takes place between the second and fourth treatment sessions, ensuring sufficient time for rapport building beforehand and supported implementation of the plan afterwards.

Typically, school refusers are unlikely to work willingly towards school return, and the task of engaging them in an intervention programme can be a challenging one for the practitioner. There is usually much at stake should children continue to miss school, and so it is important for the intervention to proceed, even if they protest or declare that they are never returning to school. The practitioner can look to foster a young person's engagement by:

➤ consistently offering empathic acknowledgement of the difficulty faced by child;
➤ cultivating a positive expectation that things will improve;
➤ making statements of confidence in the child's ability to cope and work through the problem;
➤ modelling confidence in the strategies recommended.

Some of the key components of engaging a young person in treatment are included in the 'HARD GOING' acronym (Appendix 4).

Practice tasks are an essential component of the intervention. Assigning children tasks to complete between sessions provides them with opportunities to reinforce what has been learned in-session and to practise applying these skills in the real-life setting. Children are able to report back on their experiences of using the skills, allowing for fine-tuning or trouble-shooting of any difficulties experienced. Practice tasks play a central role in facilitating the generalization of skills beyond the therapeutic context and increasing the likelihood that gains made during treatment will be maintained.

A collaborative problem-solving approach should permeate the treatment sessions with the school refuser. The practitioner should consistently engage the child in guided 'brainstorming' activities focused on anticipating challenging situations which might realistically arise, generating possible solutions to the challenging situations, considering the likely outcomes of the solutions, and deciding upon a solution (cf. Kendall *et al.*, 1992a). Emphasis should be placed on the child testing a possible solution and meeting with the practitioner to discuss the outcome.

The final treatment session

We also like to incorporate a 'Secrets to Success' activity in the final treatment session (cf. Kendall *et al.*, 1992b). This is an opportunity for the child to share ideas about how to deal effectively with a school refusal problem. It serves to reinforce what the child has learned and build up the child's coping template (Kendall *et al.*, 1992a), facilitating the maintenance of treatment gains. It also provides a more formal occasion for recognition and reward of efforts and achievements during treatment, and provides an opportunity for the child to gain some closure on the school refusal problem. The activity may take several forms, including: a poster to be displayed in the clinic; an audio-taped or video-taped mock interview in which the child plays the 'expert in the field'; a presentation in which the child instructs another practitioner or family members in the management of school refusal; or some other exercise of the child's choice.

One 12-year-old girl at the School Refusal Clinic made a poster of her 'tips' for other adolescents trying to overcome a school refusal problem. Entitled 'Allanah's Advice, the poster included the following suggestions:

➢ Will yourself to go.
➢ Taking little steps, one at a time, helps.
➢ Catch up on some work before you go back.
➢ Things aren't as bad as they seem.
➢ Practising answering questions helps.
➢ Keep in contact with friends.
➢ It's all worth it in the end.

Part IV: Intervention with the parents

Overview

Working with the parents of school refusers is predicated upon a range of factors. First, parents may inadvertently play a role in the development or maintenance of the problem. For example, good intentions associated with allowing a child to stay at home until feeling more confident to face school may ultimately serve to strengthen the child's avoidance. Secondly, many parents can be helped to manage some of the circumstances in the child's environment that may facilitate attendance. For example, management of the child's access to pleasurable events at home during school hours (e.g. watching television, going to the shops or having nice lunches) can reduce the secondary gain associated with school refusal. A third factor relates to the ongoing capacity that parents have to monitor progress and respond to early signs of relapse. Finally, parents' own anxiety about their child's capacity to cope with school attendance needs to be addressed in order that parents are not modelling and reinforcing unhelpful attitudes and behaviours in their child.

The core components of intervention with the parents include:

➤ attention to preliminary considerations;
➤ helping parents develop appropriate behaviour management strategies;
➤ facilitating the implementation of those strategies.

These components are discussed in the sections to follow.

For the most part, the content of the parent sessions follows an instructive handout. By using a handout, the parents and practitioner are helped to attend systematically to the range of strategies which are aimed at helping parents make a directed effort to return their child to regular schooling. For many parents, the handout serves to normalize their difficulties, to build confidence in the approach and to reinforce some of their previous efforts. In some cases it is wise to provide each section of the handout only as it is addressed during intervention, in an effort to prevent sceptical parents from looking at the entire handout and contesting that they have 'done all of this before and it doesn't work'.

The first intervention session begins with further rapport building, an orientation to the intervention process (e.g. that school return is scheduled mid-way through intervention) and some education about the presenting problem. Educational topics may include the development, nature and course of school refusal, anxiety and behaviour problems, together with information about the effectiveness of current approaches to treatment.

Some parents find it difficult to engage in intervention before having an answer to the question 'Why is my child like this?' It is important to acknowledge the parents' desire to have a definite answer to this question. At the same time, it is helpful for parents to learn that it is not always possible or necessary to comprehend all of the aetiological considerations before successfully helping a child cope with regular schooling. A separate handout addressing contributing factors can facilitate discussion around those factors which may be pertinent to the parents' specific situation, before moving on to the core intervention programme.

Other information conveyed to the parents at this early stage of intervention includes the following:

➢ secondary reinforcement at home can be a powerful factor in the child's refusal to attend school;
➢ a central and effective treatment for anxiety is exposure;
➢ exposure may not be initiated by the child without parental management of the child's attendance.

The need for education about school refusal, anxiety disorders and behaviour management is reflected in parents' well intentioned but often unsuccessful attempts to manage school refusal. The unsuccessful approaches typically include persuasion, punishment, bribery and seeing whether the child's refusal will dissipate over time.

Within the first (or perhaps second) session the focus moves to the first part of the handout; by this time parents are generally very eager to move on with the intervention process. Following a review of the educational information in each section of the handout, the practitioner:

➢ facilitates a discussion about the relevance of that issue for the parents and their experience in addressing that issue;
➢ encourages the parents to engage in a problem-solving discussion of how they might apply the advice covered in that section;
➢ engages the parents in active training of relevant behaviour-management strategies, employing the performance-based methods of modelling, rehearsal and feedback;
➢ challenges the parents to test the solutions and skills arising out of the problem-solving discussions and the active training.

Progress through the handout is influenced by the parents' responses to the above points. When parents display a reluctance to learn or use the strategies, the practitioner needs to explore the ambivalence, endeavouring to restructure unhelpful or irrational cognitions.

Preliminary considerations

The parent handout prompts discussion of several key issues that need to be addressed before the parents acquire and use the behaviour-management strategies.

Confidence in the child's current school placement

Parents are encouraged to discuss any doubts about their child's current school placement. A child's current school is usually convenient to the family and cooperative about plans for intervention, but occasionally a change in schools is indicated. For example, the child's relationship with peers or the family's relationship with school staff may have become so problematic that planning for attendance at the same school appears unfitting. The same principle applies to the child's placement within a particular class, with a particular teacher, or in a particular year.

When parents express doubts about their child's school or class placement, the practitioner can facilitate a problem-solving discussion aimed at helping the parents decide upon the most suitable placement for their child. Parents may be given the task of gathering further information about the various schools available to the child so that they can make a more informed decision. Some parents elect to discuss the options for school placement with the child. While being supportive of the parents' use of a consultative approach with their child, the practitioner may advise parents that some children are likely to reject all schools by virtue of their difficulty with school attendance. By anticipating scenarios like this, the practitioner may help strengthen the parents' confidence in the practitioner and their commitment to the intervention programme.

In some cases parents will already have attempted to get their child to attend one or more new schools, perhaps before adequate efforts aimed at returning their child to the original school. Alternatively, some parents express a reluctance to change schools for fear of teaching their child to 'run away from problems'. In both instances, parents are helped to evaluate, systematically and rationally, all of the concrete and potential advantages and disadvantages associated with each option for school placement.

Occasionally this problem-solving discussion will become the focus of one or two whole sessions. All the while, the practitioner aims to help the parents make a decision they are comfortable with, refraining from making a decision on their behalf.

Assessment of the child's physical health

Given that school refusers often complain about headaches, stomachaches or other somatic symptoms, and given that some may have a history of illness affecting school attendance (e.g. viral infection; chronic fatigue syndrome), parents are advised to arrange for their child to be examined by a doctor just before return to school. This aims to determine whether there is any medical basis to illness complaints. A clean bill of health is a message to the child, parents, school staff and practitioner that it is appropriate to work towards the child's return to school. Rather than harbouring doubts and anxieties about the child's health, parents can feel more confident about pursuing the plan for school return despite a child's complaints of feeling unwell. It is surmised that complaints of illness are most likely anxiety-based symptoms or, in some cases, ploys on the child's behalf to break down the parents' resolve to work towards school return.

Additional medical check-ups may be warranted through the course of an intervention in order to address recurrent uncertainties about the child's health. The medical practitioner needs to be informed of the child's difficulty with school attendance in order to prevent well meaning but unhelpful suggestions that the child remain at home until no longer experiencing any symptoms.

Strategies for facilitating school attendance

These strategies are aimed at helping parents to regain control of the situation and to ensure their child's regular attendance at school. In time, and with sufficient attention to preparation of the parents, child and school personnel, it is anticipated that the child's regular attendance will ultimately become voluntary.

Minimizing secondary gain

Parental efforts to get children off to school often result in them crying, protesting, having a tantrum or negotiating with the parents. Not being sure of what to do about such highly anxious and resistive behaviour, parents may sometimes allow children to stay at home, believing that they will eventually settle down and be better able to cope with school. Parents are helped to see that during the day children are inadvertently 'rewarded' for staying at home, thus learning that home has many advantages over school. The practitioner can suggest a range of possible rewarding aspects of being at home – the secondary gain – including the fact that children can use their time in their own way, may have access to the refrigerator, television, computer, pets, games and toys, and may also enjoy having the sole attention of a parent. The practitioner can also explain that, by staying at home, children are escaping from the school situation into familiar and comfortable surroundings, which can be quite powerful in maintaining school avoidance. Parents are encouraged to identify those aspects of home life that might be reinforcing their child's non-attendance, and to reduce those reinforcers to a minimum.

Establishing a smooth household routine

In keeping with the need to prepare the child for school return, parents are encouraged to establish a smooth household routine in the lead-up to the return, such that the routine resembles that of a regular school week. Many school refusers develop poor sleeping patterns during their absence from school, so parents are encouraged to establish a normal bedtime and waking routine. Older children may be given the opportunity to take responsibility for getting up by using an alarm clock. In the morning children are to dress for school and to engage in activities closely related to school attendance (i.e. reading and homework). Other favourite activities can be resumed only after the time at which the child would ordinarily have finished school for the day.

The message is conveyed to the child that doing school-related activities at home is a temporary arrangement until the scheduled school return; it is not an alternative to school return. Quite distinct from providing home tuition, this measure serves the dual purpose of providing the child with some home-based activity that is not too reinforcing, and helping to prepare the child for reintegration into the academic setting. However, parents are advised not to place too much emphasis at this time upon the child's performance in these school-related activities.

To help eliminate some of the hassle associated with the day of school return, parents are advised to ensure that the child's school clothes and bag are ready the night before. In cases where parents encourage their child to prepare these things and the child refuses, the parents are encouraged to make the preparations, thus conveying the message that school attendance is expected the next day. In other cases this scenario will present parents with an opportunity to practise giving instructions. The overriding principle is to prevent too much tension on the night before school return.

Clarifying the date and process for school return

Parents are helped to make a decision about an appropriate date for the child's school return and whether the child ought to begin attending full time or gradually build up time in attendance at school. In general, school return is scheduled halfway through the intervention programme. Important factors influencing the specific return date include the availability of both parents to escort the child to school, together with knowledge of the child's school timetable. In an effort to create a positive experience for the child on the first day of school return, it is helpful to plan for return on a day when the child has the least number of disliked subjects or teachers.

A return on Thursday or Friday may provide some leverage because it is soon followed by the weekend. In the case of primary students, parents often make these decisions independent of the child. However, it is felt that some therapeutic leverage may be obtained with secondary students by having parents consult with them on their preferred type of return and which weekday they prefer, while the parents still make the decision about at which stage of the intervention the child will return to school (but approximately halfway through intervention).

Giving instructions

Parents need to be absolutely clear in their communication with the child about school attendance. The question is not *if* the child attends school but *when*. Once parents have decided upon the date, they are encouraged to choose a suitable time and place to inform the child about the date of school return. This is usually best done just a few days before the return date, so as to reduce the time when the child is likely to become anxious about the event, while still giving some time to get used to the idea. Parents who are anxious about the process of informing the child can be helped to develop an 'instruction script' which is role-played with the practitioner.

Clear, firm commands can facilitate the child's compliance in situations such as getting out of bed, dressing for school, and getting in and out of the car. Instruction giving is also important in establishing a smooth household routine before the day of school return. If required, parents are taught how to give instructions effectively and calmly to the child using appropriate eye contact and body language and keeping instructions simple. Because we strongly encourage both parents to be involved in getting the child to school, it is often helpful to use the parents as co-distributors of commands. For example, if the child does not respond to mum's initial instruction to get out of bed, the consequence might be for both mum and dad to come into the room and take necessary actions such as opening the curtains, turning on some music and pulling back the blankets. In the School Refusal Clinic, a supplemental handout based upon Sanders' (1992) guidelines was employed with parents when indicated by their need to acquire more effective instruction-giving skills.

On occasion, it is likely that parents will need to back up their verbal instructions by gently, physically guiding the child to perform the required behaviour (e.g. placing a hand on the child's shoulder and guiding the child towards school clothes or the car). Parents who are ambivalent about using a firm approach are encouraged to consider whether any alternative action is likely to be effective. Frequently, parents come to realize that the firm approach may need to be tried in order to effect a change. In addition to helping with school return, a kind but firm approach can give children security. Children learn that they can rely on their parents to support them through a crisis and that their parents mean what they say.

Commitment to an approach involving parental management of school refusal behaviour is likely to be affected by the possibility of some physical harm or danger to the child or others, and the possibility of damage to property. It is important to determine the parents' ability to remain in control, and discourage aggressive responses towards the young person. In the School Refusal Clinic, we surveyed all families regarding the frequency and seriousness of any physical injuries and property damage. The very occasional reports of injury and property damage were not of a serious nature (e.g. scratches, kicked doors). The potential for personal harm and property damage highlights the need for careful planning at each stage of the child's return to school. Some appropriate preventative measures could include safety locks on car doors, the use of a 'settling in room' on arrival at school and before separation from parents, closer supervision of students who may run away from school and cross busy roads, and more school-based support for students who become extremely distressed while at school. Sensitivity to the timing and gradation of the child's school return can also reduce the child's distress and decrease the possibility of reactive and possibly injurious or dangerous behaviours.

To balance the parents' firmness in managing the child, some parents engage in one of the child's favourite activities (e.g. bowling) or to treat the child to dinner out. Increasing positive interactions between the parents and child also serves to counterbalance some of the possible negative affect generated through the parents' use of the planned ignoring strategy.

Planned ignoring

Illness complaints without physical basis, crying, protests, negotiation, or tantrums are all likely to occur when parents are being firm about school attendance. It is important that parents react in ways that help their child to cope with the situation and do not strengthen their child's refusal. Simply offering comfort and reassurance at those times when the child needs to face

the feared situation can feed into the child's problem and insecurity. There-
fore, it is recommended that parents ignore behaviours such as complaining
of feeling unwell, crying or tantrums, and the child's efforts to persuade
parents that he/she is not ready to go to school. If consistently and effectively
ignored, these behaviours are likely to decrease over time in accordance with
the principle of extinction. Training in planned ignoring may make use of a
supplemental handout drawing on Sanders' (1992) guidelines, and the training procedure includes modelling, rehearsal and feedback. Parents are also
encouraged to prompt and reinforce each other's use of the strategy at home,
and to provide constructive feedback when necessary.

It needs to be acknowledged that planned ignoring is more easily said than
done, as such behaviours are often very unpleasant for parents to endure.
Also, the child may test the parents out by protesting even more loudly,
throwing even more severe tantrums and physically resisting the parents'
efforts. At this point, parents may feel like giving up, believing that things will
not work and that it is not worth the struggle. Parents are advised not to give
up despite the discomfort they may feel, and that during this testing time
children need to be shown that the parents are confident in their ability to
cope and have no doubt that they will return to school. Parents are educated
about the 'extinction burst' – the increase in problematic behaviour which
often occurs when the behaviour is no longer reinforced. This education
process helps parents appreciate the need to be consistent in their use of
planned ignoring.

It is helpful to clarify for parents that offering comfort and reassurance to
the child are not being disregarded in the implementation. A distinction is
made between the times at which planned ignoring is best employed (i.e. in
the mornings before school) and the times when it is appropriate and helpful
for parents to listen to their child's concerns and to play a more comforting
role (i.e. after school hours and on the weekend). Suggest that planned
ignoring can be implemented in a supportive way, by incorporating messages
about the parents' care for the child. Such messages are best planned and
rehearsed. For example, a parent may respond to a child's attempts to
negotiate school attendance in the following way:

> Peter, I understand that you feel nervous and I care about the way you feel. I also
> know that it will get easier for you once you're back at school. For now, your job is to
> get ready for school. We won't be talking about these things anymore this morning.
> When you come home from school we'll talk some more. Now go and put your
> school shoes on please.

Any further negotiation by the child is completely ignored, as planned.

Modelling confidence

The morning of school return is often very stressful for parents as well as children. Discussion takes place around the fact that children learn a great deal through watching others, that parents are probably the most important role models in their children's life, and that if children see their parents being anxious and agitated when faced with a difficult situation they too may learn to respond in that way. Conversely, parents' confidence and definite expectation that children are going to school can provide a good role model. If parents are relatively calm, relaxed and in control, children have a model which may help them overcome their anxiety and fear.

Statements such as 'I know you can do it' and 'You've done it before, you can do it again' convey parental confidence and encourage the child to confront rather than avoid the source of anxiety. Parents can also model the use of their own coping statements in other difficult situations, demonstrating for the child that it is legitimate and potentially helpful to prompt themselves to 'stay as calm as possible' for example, or to remember that 'it's okay to feel a bit uptight; it doesn't mean I can't handle this challenge'.

Parents are encouraged to generate some appropriate coping statements they can use to help themselves stay calm while managing the child's school attendance. More anxious parents may be encouraged to think about additional strategies that they can use to calm themselves in challenging situations. Some parents might benefit from training in controlled breathing so that they can address their own physiological anxiety when returning their child to school.

Escorting the child to school

One of the most instrumental factors in helping children face and overcome fear is to block avoidance behaviour and expose them to the feared situation. In the context of school refusal this constitutes being taken to school. Initially, two people should escort the child – preferably both parents. Seeing both parents acting together can give the child a feeling of security. Often the father's involvement in escorting is novel, perhaps requiring him to rearrange work commitments, thus emphasizing the seriousness of the parents' intent to return the child to school. The involvement of both parents also means that they can support each other in what may be a difficult situation.

If it is not possible to involve two parents in escorting, then it is suggested that one parent is helped by another person such as a relative, neighbour or friend. The involvement of school staff is usually discouraged in order to prevent them from becoming aversive to the child. Practitioners are not usually involved in the procedure for the same reason and in order to ensure that parents can develop the skills for managing their child's behaviour independent of the practitioner. In a few cases, however, initial leverage in helping the child return to school is achieved through the direct involvement of school staff or practitioners in the escorting procedure. The 'pros' and 'cons' need to be weighed up before such an approach is adopted (e.g. unavailability of another parent, relative or friend; availability of school staff or practitioner; possibility that the parent seeks to relinquish responsibility for managing the child's attendance).

In almost every case, the escorting procedure represents the crux of the intervention for parents. This is the point in their previous attempts to return the child to school that has been most challenging and unsuccessful. Usually, having the supportive guidance of the practitioner is sufficient to prompt parents to attempt to return their child to school again. In some cases parents need to be helped to compare previous failed attempts with the current approach, exposing the fact that the parents and school are now much better prepared to manage the child's school return.

Parents are advised that the child's imminent exposure to the feared situation is likely to lead to protest, tantrums and complain of illness. At this time parents need to draw upon their acquired knowledge and skills (i.e. instruction giving; planned ignoring; modelling confidence) and firmly proceed with managing their child's attendance by escorting the child to school.

Leaving the child at school

After successfully getting the child to school, another hurdle is leaving the child there. This is likely to be a stressful time for the child and it can lead to feelings of guilt and worry for parents. Parents are advised to arrive at school at a specified time and place. In some cases this involves the parents escorting the child to a nominated staff member shortly after the other children have gone into class, so as to reduce the chance that the child will be embarrassed in front of peers, especially if he/she appears very anxious. In other cases, usually involving adolescents, parents have consulted with their child about which arrangement would be easiest (e.g. walking alone from the car to the student welfare coordinator's office; going straight into the first class of the day; having a staff member come to the car).

Parents are encouraged to keep parting comments brief and firm, carrying the expectation that the child will cope (e.g. 'Bye now Paul. Have a good day. See you at 3.30'). If the child cries or tantrums when being left at school, parents are to remain calm and proceed to leave the school. They are informed that the signs of distress shown by school refusers are not necessarily indications that the child will not be able to cope at school, and that, after parents have left, children often settle down quickly. They are also reminded that the school assumes responsibility for the child's welfare and that the school staff have been prepared to handle the child's return to school. While at school, it is usually best if the child is not contacted by the parents, or else the parents may fail to model confidence in the child's ability to cope and may arouse the child's anxiety (e.g. about being away from mum and dad).

Sometimes leaving the child at school presents parents and school staff with more of a challenge than escorting the child to school. It may be extremely difficult to get children out of the car or to stop them clinging to their parents once inside the school building. When it is considered inappropriate to address these problems by physically moving the child (e.g. due to the child's size, parents' values, or school policy), alternative strategies can be employed. Parents can stay with the child in an inconspicuous and uninteresting place in the school building or in the car as necessary, using planned ignoring. In this way the child is desensitized to the school setting while learning that the consequence of refusing to comply is staying at school; the avoidance of school is prohibited. Moreover, the option of complying and entering the classroom becomes increasingly attractive as parents persist in their use of planned ignoring. Parents are advised that this approach requires great patience, as it may take several hours or even days before the child will opt to enter the classroom.

Dealing with running away

If children run away from school, it is essential that they are returned immediately. This continues the blocking of avoidance behaviour, and the child is more likely to learn that there is no point in running away. Although it is uncommon, parents need to prepare for this possibility and remember that immediate action is required. School staff need to be kept updated with the parents' contact numbers during the day, so as to notify them quickly of the child's absence. If either parent is unavailable to return the child to school, they should make plans for a family friend or relative to do this.

Positive reinforcement

Positive reinforcement is an integral part of the intervention, aimed at increasing desired behaviours in the child such as preparing for school, attending school, or using coping skills – essentially any effort the child makes to tackle and cope with school attendance. Because of its importance, considerable time is spent helping parents appreciate the potential value of appropriately administering positive reinforcement. This is especially relevant when parents berate positive reinforcement because they perceive it as bribery or have had questionable success in using it at other times. Moreover, it is often too easy for some parents to downplay the child's small achievements because they fall short of the parents' own hopes or expectations regarding the rate of improvement.

Discussion centres on the effective administration of rewards, such as the importance of selecting potent rewards and ones that can be provided immediately after the desired behaviour occurs. As a practice task between sessions, parents are often encouraged to generate a menu of tangible rewards and privileges. It is suggested that rewards be paired with social praise. It should be explained that the naturally occurring reinforcers (e.g. academic success at school; re-establishing friendships) can ultimately replace the need for contrived reinforcement.

Children are ideally reinforced for something on each of the first few days of attempted school return. The schedule of reinforcement is gradually modified over time, such that children are reinforced for two consecutive days of attendance, and then three, and so on. In some cases reinforcement contracts are developed between the parents and child. This approach to reinforcing the child is avoided when the parents' knowledge of the child suggests that the child would not be engaged in the process, in which case rewards are administered spontaneously as opposed to contractually.

At the same time as the use of positive reinforcement recognizes children's efforts and encourages them to try again the next day, it also gives them a chance to develop a positive view of themselves, as they are reminded of the things they have done well. It thus serves to counterbalance the parents' use of other strategies, such as planned ignoring and escorting to school.

Some parents will express concern that they are being unfair to their other children by focusing attention on the school refuser and that this may create problems among the siblings. An opportunity exists for parents to consider employing positive reinforcement for appropriate behaviours noticed in their other children. This has the added advantage of helping the school refuser see that positive behaviours are acknowledged and reinforced.

Facilitating the process

Cognitive restructuring

The practitioner needs to listen carefully to parental beliefs and attitudes associated with the management of school refusal. Cognitive restructuring is employed when parents display cognitions that are likely to have a negative impact upon their engagement in the intervention process and their implementation of the strategies (cf. Anderson *et al.*, 1998). Unhelpful cognitions are detected throughout treatment, inferred from parents' statements and behaviours or elicited via specific questioning. They may also be detected during the initial assessment phase.

The unhelpful cognitions may reflect, among other things, low self-efficacy (e.g. 'there is nothing I can do which will get my child back to school'), hopelessness (e.g. 'I don't think anything can work anymore'), relinquished responsibility (e.g. 'it's up to the school to make the difference now'; 'my son has to want to go to school before anything will change'), guilt (e.g. 'I should have sent her to another school in the first place'; 'we should have tried to get help earlier'), black-and-white thinking (e.g. 'it's wrong to force a child to do anything'), catastrophizing (e.g. 'my child will become depressed if I stop him doing the things he wants to do when he's not at school'), and selective attention or memory (e.g. 'my child has made no improvements whatsoever, nothing has changed'). To the extent that such styles of thinking have a negative impact upon parent engagement and effort, they need to be addressed during intervention.

In large part the restructuring of unhelpful cognitions is achieved via Socratic questioning, which encourages parents:

➢ to weigh up the evidence that supports and disconfirms the belief;
➢ to develop alternative ways of thinking about the situation;
➢ to consider the advantages and disadvantages of holding the belief;
➢ to consider the advantages and disadvantages of alternative behaviour management practices.

Some of the additional cognitive restructuring techniques may include the 'awfulizing scale', the use of metaphor and behavioural experiments (see McMullin, 2000). Parents may be challenged to act 'as if' they believe the behaviour management strategies might be appropriate and effective, the aim being to attenuate unhelpful beliefs via a change in the parents' (successful) use of the strategies. When working with two parents it is often very helpful to elicit the ideas of the parent whose thoughts seem to be more adaptive, because the other parent is regularly observed to assimilate these ideas.

At a more fundamental level, informal cognitive restructuring occurs throughout the entire intervention programme as parents are helped to see new ways to handle old problems.

Modelling, rehearsal and feedback

As previously mentioned, the performance-based methods of modelling, rehearsal and feedback are used during parent training in behaviour management strategies. This approach provides the parents with opportunities to gain confidence and increase their competence in the use of the strategies. With increased confidence and competence, parents are more likely to employ the strategies, and to employ them effectively. In turn, the experience of using the strategies effectively increases the likelihood that parents will persist in their use of these and other strategies as required; self-efficacy is enhanced. An essential component of the in-session practice of skills is the opportunity it affords the practitioner to observe directly, and provide positive and constructive feedback. Relying on parents' reports of their practice or use of the strategies may only perpetuate the ineffective use of the strategy. For example, parents have said to us that they thought they were using planned ignoring at home, but after role-playing in-session they could see that they were in fact giving attention to the child's tantrums.

The performance-based method relies on the parents and practitioner rehearsing possible scenarios, often in the context of structured role-plays (e.g. the practitioner playing the role of the child whining about having to return to school, and then trying to negotiate with the parents about returning at some time other than that nominated by the parents). Initially, this may be quite discomforting for the parents (and even the practitioner). It is useful to acknowledge the discomfort that may be felt and to make initial role-plays relatively brief and easy. As the process becomes more familiar, the scenarios can be made longer and more challenging, and thus more realistic.

In some cases, rehearsal of the strategies may be incorporated in a more seamless fashion into the discourse of the session, without any mention of 'role-plays' or 'practice'. For example, the practitioner may simply ask how the parents would respond to the child complaining that he/she was not ready to go to school on the morning of the planned school return. Depending on the response, the practitioner would follow up with other questions or comments. This seamless approach is particularly indicated when the practitioner's knowledge of the parents suggests that efforts to engage them in role-play scenarios would jeopardize the therapeutic relationship.

Parents are encouraged to complete between-session tasks as a means of practising new skills and effecting change. At one level, practice tasks accelerate the therapeutic process by encouraging parents to engage in further discussion or practice of those things covered during the session. For example, parents may be asked to give some consideration to possible rewards to be included in a reward menu or, beyond that, to establish a hierarchy of rewards contingent upon specific achievements by the child. Further, parents may be asked to practise planned ignoring between sessions. In the process, practice tasks facilitate the generalization of the skills to situations outside the clinical setting. By following up on the parents' completion (or otherwise) of the practice tasks, the practitioner emphasizes the value of the tasks, and has an opportunity to reinforce parental efforts or to explore reasons for the non-completion of the tasks and to adapt them as necessary.

The highly anxious child

When a child displays a very high level of anxiety, parents may be helped to implement an exposure hierarchy before school return. For example, children anxious about separation could be exposed to increasing periods of separation from mum and dad, and socially anxious children could be provided with opportunities to engage in social interactions with other children. Together, the practitioner and parents establish appropriate fear hierarchies, and the parents play a central role in prompting and reinforcing the child's progress through the steps of the hierarchy between sessions. This preliminary desensitization is aimed at better preparing the child for the return to school.

The final intervention session

The final intervention session focuses upon relapse prevention via a review of the programme contents. Particular attention is given to those strategies found to be most useful, together with discussion about high-risk times, indications of impending relapse and appropriate responses.

Supporting parents

Throughout intervention, parents seek and value a high level of practitioner support, particularly if they are contending with their own emotional distress. In the process, the practitioner needs to pay close attention to the smallest signs of progress, as these are often overlooked by distressed parents and by parents with unrealistic expectations of their child. The beginning of each session provides an opportunity to review and reinforce progress, and to fine-tune the intervention plan as necessary. Parents are invited to telephone the practitioner at any stage during the intervention. Contact is mostly made because the child's return to school did not go according to plan. At this time the practitioner needs to provide support for the distressed parents, reinforce their efforts and sensitively facilitate a problem-solving discussion aimed at modifying and reimplementing the plan.

Part V: Intervention at the school level

Overview

Intervention with parents is complemented with school consultation, the aims being to ensure consistency of management between the caregivers and to facilitate the child's smooth transition into regular school attendance. At least one school visit is ideally scheduled before the child's school return, followed by regular telephone contact. Telephone contact with school personnel after the consultative visit focuses on trouble-shooting and the maintenance of treatment gains.

Like the parent programme, the school consultation involves education and the facilitation of a problem-solving approach to helping the child cope with school return.

Strategies for managing school refusal

Before arrival

The specific date for the child's school return is discussed with school staff, taking into account its convenience to both the parents and the staff. Subsequently, all relevant staff are to be informed of the arrangements for the child's return. A memo may be circulated to ensure that staff are suitably informed. When appropriate, the child's peers may also be informed of the child's return to school, and advised to be supportive and to refrain from probing the child about the absence, which can be a particularly anxiety-provoking experience and a major factor in school avoidance (King et al., 1995). The decision to inform peers is based upon the teacher's estimation of the peers' likely support for the child, together with the child's expressed wishes.

On arrival

It is recommended that one or two staff members be available to meet with the child on arrival at school, ideally the staff member(s) most liked by the child. This should be at the time and place prearranged with the parents, specially chosen so as to avoid making the child's arrival at school a highly visible event to peers and other staff, thereby reducing embarrassment and anxiety.

Staff are encouraged to greet the child in a positive and friendly manner, resisting the temptation to express disappointment in the child's behaviour, or asking for an explanation about the absence from school. Commonly, children are upset on arrival at school or when the parents leave, and so a place may be chosen where the child can spend time with the nominated staff member(s) and begin to settle down before going into class. Again, an inconspicuous and quiet location is preferred. Some children are worried about what might be expected of them academically, or about mixing with the other children. The staff member(s) can allay distress by explaining how the child will be accommodated academically and socially, and by explaining the general plan for the day.

Reintroduction to class

Graded reintroduction to classes and school routines is recommended for children who have been absent for some time, and for those who have particular difficulty with a certain aspect of school. For example, children may be specially accommodated by excusing them from physical education class or school assembly, by setting a reduced homework load, or by refraining from asking them questions in front of the class. The child phobic of the classroom situation may initially be accommodated in the school counsellor's office and then in a classroom with a small number of students. As children settle back into regular school attendance, the special arrangements can gradually be withdrawn until they are fully involved in normal school life. Of course, some students require ongoing support in academic or other areas.

Staff are encouraged to select one or two suitable peers who can be 'special buddies' to help with children's social and academic integration. In the classroom, buddies may sit with them, help them with class work, and select them for group activities. Between classes, buddies may involve them in activities, support them in the face of potential conflict, and help secondary college students in particular to make sense of the timetable and to find their way around the school.

Dealing with resistance

Throughout the school day school refusers might complain of feeling unwell and plead to be allowed to go home. Staff are encouraged to ignore inappropriate behaviours such as these, employing the same supportive yet consistent approach as outlined for parents. The staff need to be informed of the child's physical health based on the medical examination arranged by the parents, in order that they can feel more confident about ignoring complaints of illness. On some occasions children are genuinely physically unwell at school. When school staff are able to accommodate minor illnesses in the sick bay, school staff and parents are encouraged to keep the child at school.

Another behaviour that is managed in part by planned ignoring is the child's asking to be able to telephone home. In some instances allowing the child to make a specified number of telephone calls home (e.g. one call per day) helps to increase the child's rapport with staff and diminishes the child's experience of school as an aversive place. This strategy is employed only when parents have been prepared to respond to the child's telephone calls in a helpful manner, by prompting the child to employ coping strategies for example. Beyond the agreed number of telephone calls, staff are advised to ignore the child's further requests to telephone home.

A few school refusers attempt to leave school during the day. Consequently, children need to be observed very carefully in the first few weeks of school return. Staff are encouraged to develop a plan for monitoring the child's attendance during class time and between classes. If the child succeeds in running away from school it is usually to the security of the home. Staff are to contact the parents, whether they be at home or work, so that they can return the child to school immediately.

Strong emphasis is placed upon the provision of suitable positive re-inforcement for children's appropriate behaviour (i.e. school attendance; use of coping skills). In addition to increasing the likelihood of the behaviour recurring and helping children develop a favourable view of themselves, this strategy serves to make the school environment more inviting for the wary refuser. If staff have difficulty generating ideas for school-based reinforce-ments, the practitioner may offer suggestions based upon the responses of staff at other schools. Special privileges are often more easily arranged than tangible reinforcement. These may include extra time on the computer, running errands for the teacher, choosing an activity for the class, or 10 minutes of extra break time with a group of friends.

Facilitating the process

Generally, we have found staff to be very cooperative about plans for facili-tating the child's return to school. Sometimes, in light of the increased pressures upon schools with reduced resources, staff might be ambivalent about investing the time and effort suggested by the intervention. To stimu-late cooperation, the consultation begins with a review of the assessment findings that highlight the child's need for support. Moreover, the instructive handout pre-empts common questions about the recommended strategies, aimed at helping staff to appreciate:

> ➤ that the special arrangements are time limited;
> ➤ that school refusers commonly display emotional upset on arrival at school, lest the staff fear that their use of the strategies may be inappropriate with children who are upset, discouraging them from using the strategies;
> ➤ that the consistent use of the strategies reduces the risk of long-term social and emotional difficulties if the child were to continue refusing to attend school.

Close liaison between the parents and the school is encouraged. As the intervention progresses, the practitioner can provide an increasing number of opportunities for these two parties to negotiate the necessary arrangements without the mediation of the practitioner (e.g. determining when the child would progress from four classes per day to six classes per day, or when to increase expectations about the completion of homework). It is anticipated that the development of a collaborative approach between the two parties helps to ward off relapse, or helps them to respond efficiently and effectively to the signs of relapse. Consistent with the work with parents, school staff are advised about possible high-risk times for relapse and the indicators of impending relapse, and they are encouraged to employ the current strategies should a relapse occur.

Part VI: Concluding remarks

As well as causing distress for young people and their families, school refusal poses a significant challenge for staff within education, mental health and welfare settings. In our time at the School Refusal Clinic, the challenge has sometimes become frustrating and demoralizing. The support, inspiration and expertise of colleagues have been invaluable in helping us effectively support school refusers, their parents and school personnel. Ultimately, we have found that the persistent and patient application of the intervention strategies outlined in this guide has been instrumental in helping many families.

The most challenging scenarios have tended to involve school refusers over 14 years of age for whom school attendance has been a long-standing problem. Our research suggests that the cognitive-behavioural approach can be of assistance to some of these children, but that many do not return to regular and voluntary school attendance. This finding is very much in keeping with those reported by others (e.g. King et al., 1995). Further empirical research is required in order to determine which of the older, chronic school refusers are more likely to benefit from a cognitive-behavioural intervention. Predictor analyses may also shed light on the effect of comorbid diagnoses (such as depression), parental psychopathology and family dysfunction on the outcome of a cognitive-behavioural intervention. In some cases, booster sessions, alternative psychosocial interventions or adjunctive pharmacological interventions may be indicated. For now, little research support exists for these alternative approaches.

References

Achenbach, T.M. (1991a). *Manual for the Child Behavior Checklist/4-18 and 1991 Profile*. Burlington, VT: University of Vermont Department of Psychiatry.

Achenbach, T.M. (1991b). *Manual for the Teacher's Report Form and 1991 Profile*. Burlington, VT: University of Vermont Department of Psychiatry.

Anderson, J., King, N., Tonge, B., Rollings, S., Young, D., and Heyne, D. (1998). Cognitive-behavioural intervention for an adolescent school refuser: a comprehensive approach. *Behaviour Change, 15,* 67–73.

Berg, I. (1996). School avoidance, school phobia, and truancy. In: M. Lewis (Ed.), *Child and Adolescent Psychiatry: A Comprehensive Textbook* (pp. 1104–1110). Baltimore, MD: Williams and Wilkins.

Berg, I., Butler, A., Franklin, J., Hayes, H., Lucas, C., and Sims, R. (1993). DSM-III-R disorders, social factors and management of school attendance problems in the normal population. *Journal of Child Psychology and Psychiatry, 34,* 1187–1203.

Berg, I., Nichols, K., and Pritchard, C. (1969). School phobia: its classification and relationship to dependency. *Journal of Child Psychology and Psychiatry, 10,* 123–141.

Bernard, M. and Joyce, M. (1984). *Rational-Emotive Therapy with Children and Adolescents: Theory, Treatment Strategies, Preventative Methods.* New York: Wiley Interscience.

Blagg, N. (1987). *School Phobia and its Treatment.* New York: Croom-Helm.

Bools, C., Foster, J., Brown, I., and Berg, I. (1990). The identification of psychiatric disorders in children who fail to attend school: a cluster analysis of a non-clinical population. *Psychological Medicine, 20,* 171–181.

Broadwin, I.T. (1932). A contribution to the study of truancy. *American Journal of Orthopsychiatry, 2,* 253–259.

Burke, A.E. and Silverman, W.K. (1987). The prescriptive treatment of school refusal. *Clinical Psychology Review, 7,* 353–362.

Clarke, G., Lewinsohn, P. and Hops, H. (1990). *Student Workbook: Adolescent Coping with Depression Course.* Eugene, OR: Castalia Publishing Company.

Daugherty, T.K. and Shapiro, S.K. (1994). Behavior Checklists and Rating Forms. In: T.H. Ollendick, N.J. King and W.R. Yule (Eds.) *International Handbook of Phobic and Anxiety Disorders in Children and Adolescents* (pp. 331–346). New York: Plenum Press.

Gordon, D.A. and Young, R.D. (1976). School phobia: a discussion of aetiology, treatment and evaluation. *Psychological Reports, 39,* 783–804.

Gullone, E. and King, N. (1992). Psychometric evaluation of a revised fear survey schedule for children and adolescents. *Journal of Child Psychology and Psychiatry, 33,* 987–998.

Hersov, L. (1985). School refusal. In: M. Rutter and L. Hersov (Eds.), *Child and Adolescent Psychiatry: Modern Approaches* (2nd edn, pp. 382–399). Oxford: Blackwell.

Heyne, D. (1999). *Evaluation of Child Therapy and Caregiver Training in the Treatment of School Refusal.* Dissertation. Melbourne: Monash University.

Heyne, D., King, N., Tonge, B., Rollings, S., Pritchard, M., Young, D. and Myerson, N. (1998). The Self-Efficacy Questionnaire for School Situations: development and psychometric evaluation. *Behaviour Change, 15,* 31–40.

Holmbeck, G.N., Colder, C., Shapera, W., Westhoven, V., Kenealy, L. and Updegrove, A. (2000). Working with adolescents: guides from developmental psychology. In: P.C. Kendall (Ed.), *Child and Adolescent Therapy: Cognitive-Behavioral Procedures* (2nd edn, pp. 334–385). New York: Guilford Press.

Johnson, A.M., Falstein, E.I., Szurek, S.A. and Svendsen, M. (1941). School phobia. *American Journal of Orthopsychiatry, 11,* 702–711.

Kearney, C.A. and Albano, A.M. (2000). *When Children Refuse School: A Cognitive-Behavioral Therapy Approach – Therapist Guide.* USA: TherapyWorks. [need town??????]

Kearney, C.A. and Silverman, W.K. (1993). Measuring the function of school refusal behavior: the School Refusal Assessment Scale. *Journal of Clinical Child Psychology, 22,* 85–96.

Kendall, P.C. (1992). *Coping Cat Workbook.* Ardmore, PA: Workbook Publishing.

Kendall, P.C., Chansky, T.E., Kane, M.T., Kim, R.S., Kortlander, E., Ronan, K.R., Sessa, F.M. and Siqueland, L. (1992a). *Anxiety Disorders in Youth: Cognitive-Behavioral Interventions.* Boston: Allyn and Bacon.

Kendall, P.C., Kane, M., Howard, B. and Siqueland, L. (1992b). *Cognitive-Behavioral Therapy for Anxious Children: Therapist Manual*. Philadelphia: Workbook Publishing.

King, N.J. and Ollendick, T.H. (1989). School refusal: graduated and rapid behavioural treatment strategies. *Australian and New Zealand Journal of Psychiatry*, *23*, 213–223.

King, N.J., Ollendick, T.H. and Tonge, B.J. (1995). *School Refusal: Assessment and Treatment*. Boston: Allyn and Bacon.

King, N.J., Ollendick, T.H., Tonge, B.J., Heyne, D., Pritchard, M., Rollings, S., Young, D. and Myerson, N. (1996). Behavioural management of school refusal. *Scandinavian Journal of Behaviour Therapy*, *25*, 3–15.

Kleinknecht, R.A. and Bernstein, D.A. (1988). Fear Thermometer. In: M. Hersen and A.S. Bellack (Eds.), *Dictionary of Behavioral Assessment Techniques* (pp. 220–221). New York: Pergamon Press.

Koeppen, A.S. (1974). Relaxation training for children. *Elementary School Guidance and Counseling*, *9*, 14–21.

Kovacs, M. (1981). Rating scales to assess depression in school-aged children. *Acta Paedopsychiatrica*, *46*, 305–315.

Last, C.G. and Strauss, C.C. (1990). School refusal in anxiety-disordered children and adolescents. *Journal of the American Academy of Child and Adolescent Psychiatry*, *29*, 31–35.

McGrath, J. and Francey, S. (1991). *Friendly Kids, Friendly Classrooms: Teaching Social Skills and Confidence in the Classroom*. Melbourne: Longman Cheshire.

McMullin, R. (2000). *The New Handbook of Cognitive Therapy Techniques*. New York: W.W. Norton.

Ollendick, T.H. and Cerny, J.A. (1981). *Clinical Behavior Therapy with Children*. New York: Plenum Press.

Ollendick, T.H. and King, N.J. (1990). School phobia and separation anxiety. In: H. Leitenberg (Ed.), *Handbook of Social and Evaluation Anxiety* (pp. 179–214). New York: Plenum Press.

Ollendick, T.H. and King, N.J. (1998). Assessment practices and issues with school-refusing children. *Behaviour Change*, *15*, 16–30.

Ollendick, T.H. and Mayer, J.A. (1984). School phobia. In: S.M. Turner (Ed.), *Behavioral Treatment of Anxiety Disorders* (pp. 367–411). New York: Plenum Press.

Rapee, R., Spence, S., Cobham, V. and Wignall, A. (2000). *Helping Your Anxious Child: A Step-by-Step Guide for Parents*. Oakland, CA: New Harbinger Publications.

Reynolds, C.R. and Paget, K.D. (1983). National normative and reliability data for the Revised Children's Manifest Anxiety Scale. *School Psychology Review*, *12*, 324–336.

Reynolds, C.R. and Richmond, B.O. (1978). 'What I think and feel': a revised measure of children's manifest anxiety. *Journal of Abnormal Child Psychology*, *6*, 271–280.

Sanders, M.R. (1992). *Every Parent: A Positive Approach to Children's Behaviour*. Sydney: Addison-Wesley.

Silverman, W.K. and Albano, A.M. (1996). *Anxiety Disorders Interview Schedule for DSM–IV: Child Version, Parent Interview Schedule*. San Antonio, TX: Psychological Corporation.

Spence, S. (1995). *Social Skills Training: User's Guide*. Windsor: NFER-Nelson.

Straus, M.B. (1999). *No-Talk Therapy for Children and Adolescents*. New York: W.W. Norton.

Appendix 1. Clinical Interview Schedule – Child Version

General

Interests

➤ What do you like to do in your spare time?
➤ Do you belong to any clubs, play sports or have lessons in certain things?

Family

➤ Who else is in your family?
➤ With whom do you get on best? With whom do you get on least?
➤ What sorts of things does your family like to do together?
➤ Does your family spend time discussing things together?

Friends

➤ Who are your friends? Do they go to your school?
➤ What do you like to do with your friends at school?
➤ At break time and lunchtime, are you usually with other kids or are you on your own?
➤ Do you prefer to be on your own or do you like to be with other kids?
➤ Do you see your school friends outside school hours? What do you do with them?
➤ Do you have friends who don't go to your school?
➤ How often do you get together with friends?
➤ Would you like to have more friends?

School situation

General

➤ What school do you go to?
➤ Is that a big school or a small school?
➤ How many year (child's grade level) classes are there?
➤ How long have you attended this school? Where were you before that?
➤ Do you think your school is a good school? What are some good things about your school?
➤ What are some not-so-good things about school?
➤ Who is your (favourite) teacher? What do you like about him/her?
➤ What would you most like to do when you finish school?
➤ What do you think you *will* do when you finish school?

➢ How far do you think you will go with your schooling?

Transition to secondary school (adolescents)

➢ Which primary school did you attend?
➢ Did you enjoy primary school? What was the best thing about primary school?
➢ How was it decided which high school you would go to? Did you pick? Did mum and dad decide? Were you happy with the decision?
➢ Did any of your friends from primary school go with you to secondary school?
➢ Were you looking forward to going to secondary school? Were you nervous?
➢ Was it easy/hard getting used to secondary school?
➢ What were/are the differences between secondary school and primary school?
➢ If you could, would you prefer to be back at primary school?
➢ Did you make new friends at secondary school?
➢ How long did it take to make friends at secondary school?

Schoolwork

➢ What subjects do you do?
➢ What subjects do you enjoy?
➢ Which are your least favourite subjects?
➢ Is the work hard or easy?
➢ Do you get homework? Do you do your homework?

Behaviour at school

➢ Do you usually do what you're supposed to do at school?
➢ If you were to get into trouble at school, what would it be for?
➢ What happens if you do the wrong things in class/at school?

School refusal

➢ What do you understand about why mum and dad have brought you along today?
➢ How long have you not been at school?
➢ Is it a problem for you not being at school? Do other people see it as a problem?
➢ What does mum/dad say about you not being at school?
➢ Have you had contact with teachers from school since you stopped going?
➢ Are you doing any schoolwork at home?

➤ What sorts of things are you doing during the day at the moment?
➤ Who else is home during the day?
➤ What are the best things about being at home?
➤ What is the worst thing about not being at school?
➤ What sorts of things have made it hard for you to go to school?
➤ Did something happen at the time that you stopped going to school?
➤ What sorts of things have been tried to get you back to school?
➤ What sorts of things do you think should be tried to get you back to school?
➤ What do you think will happen if nothing is done about you not being at school?
➤ If you could change one thing about school what would it be?
➤ If you *had* to go to school tomorrow and there was no getting out of it, what would be the hardest thing for you to face?
➤ Have you ever thought about changing to another school? What would be good about that? What would be hard about doing that?
➤ Do you still have contact with your friends now that you're not at school?

Morning scenario

Getting ready
➤ What time do you wake up?
➤ Who wakes you up? How do you feel when you wake up?
➤ What do you think about when you first wake up?
➤ What do you do next after you wake up? And then what?
➤ Are you fast or slow getting ready? Does someone have to tell you to hurry up?
➤ How do you feel when you're getting ready?
➤ Who else is at home in the mornings before school?
➤ Do you ever feel nervous/scared/worried in the mornings before school?
➤ Do you ever feel sick in the mornings before school?
➤ What sort of sick feelings do you have? Have you been to the doctor to have these sick feelings/stomach pains/headaches checked out?
➤ How long do the sick feelings last? All day or do they go away during the day? About what time does the sick feeling go away?
➤ What happens on a morning that you don't feel like going to school?
➤ Does mum/dad try to make you get up and get ready for school?
➤ What does she/he say or do to try to get you to go to school?
➤ What do you do when they do/say that?
➤ Do you ever cry and get upset in the mornings before school?
➤ How does it all end up?

Going to school

➢ How do you get to school?
➢ How do you feel on the way to school?
➢ What do you think about on the way to school?
➢ Would you go if mum and dad were not around to make you go?

Worries

Some of the young people I see have stopped going to school because they (select appropriate situations):

➢ have been given a hard time by other kids at school;
➢ are worried about being left on their own at school;
➢ are worried about being away from their mother;
➢ have been really scared by their teacher yelling;
➢ are worried about their schoolwork or taking tests;
➢ are worried about having to do things in front of the class;
➢ are worried about having to use the toilets at school;
➢ are worried about having to do physical education lessons at school because they're not very good at it or they don't like getting changed into their physical education uniform at school;

Has this ever been a problem for you?

Appendix 2. Clinical Interview Schedule – Parent Version

School refusal

➢ What do you consider to be at the heart of the problem?
➢ How has the school refusal affected you/the family?

History of the school refusal

➢ When did this episode of school refusal start?
➢ How was the child last year, generally?
➢ How did the child cope with nursery school/each successive year of schooling?
➢ Have there been previous episodes of school refusal? When were these?
➢ How does the child appear towards the end of the school holidays?
➢ Has there been any running away from home/school?

Description of the school refusal
- How is the child on the night before school/on school mornings?
- How does your child get to school?
- What is the child's level of attendance/absenteeism?
- Is there a pattern of non-attendance (e.g. specific times of day/days of week/times in year)?
- How does your child come across when faced with attendance – signs of anxiety/depression/oppositional behaviour?
- Are there problems with sleeping/eating/bowel and bladder?
- Has there been a medical assessment of symptoms?
- Is your child currently on any medications for school refusal or other difficulties?

Contributing/maintaining factors
- How would you explain your child's absences – what led to them?
- Have there been distressing events during the holidays?
- Have there been changes at home (e.g. relational, financial, pet dying)?
- Has the child reported difficulty with aspects of school (e.g. bullying, teachers, schoolwork, etc)?
- What does your child do during the day, when not at school?
- How do you respond to the child when anxious/depressed/oppositional?

Attempt(s) to resolve the problem and outcomes:
- What other help has the family received?
- What has worked, and what hasn't been so helpful?
- What role has each parent played in managing the problem?

About the child

Other problems
- What other physical or psychological problems has the child experienced?
- What developmental (present or past) problems has the child experienced? How severe were these problems and how were they resolved?

Schooling
- How many schools has the child attended?
- When did the child start at the current school?
- What has the child's attitude to schooling (academic/career ambitions) been like?

Behaviour

- ➤ What is the child's behaviour like at home/school, in general?
- ➤ What changes have you noticed in your child's behaviour since refusing to attend?

Socially

- ➤ How much time does your child spend with school friends outside school?
- ➤ How much time does your child spend with other children not at the same school?
- ➤ What's the nature/quality of this social involvement?
- ➤ Does your child find it easy/hard to make and keep valuable friendships?
- ➤ Are any of your child's friends school refusers or truants?

About the parents

- ➤ What are some of your memories of being at school?
- ➤ Did you like/dislike school?
- ➤ How far did you go with your schooling?
- ➤ What are your thoughts about your child's school/teacher?
- ➤ Were there ever times when you were anxious about attending school, or truanted?
- ➤ Do you experience, or have you ever experienced, high anxiety/very low mood/other difficulties?

Family issues

- ➤ Are there other children in the family with attendance difficulties?
- ➤ How does your child get along with his/her siblings?
- ➤ How would you describe the relationship between yourself and your child?
- ➤ How would you describe your child's relationship with your partner?
- ➤ How are things for you and your partner?
- ➤ Has your child ever been separated from you/your partner for any length of time?

Treatment issues

- ➤ What general and specific changes would you like to see?
- ➤ What solutions do you think should be tried?
- ➤ What expectations do the parents have of the practitioner/setting?
- ➤ What other assistance is currently received by the child/parents?
- ➤ Which people provide the greatest support for you?

Appendix 3. Fear Thermometer

Name:
Date:

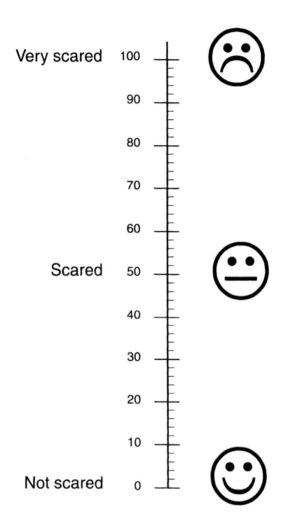

➤ Think about your worst day over the past two school weeks. How afraid
 were you of going to school on that day?
➤ How scared would you be about going to school tomorrow?

Appendix 4. The *HARD GOING* acronym

Establishing a working relationship with a client can be challenging at the best of times. The task may be particularly hard going when working with adolescent school refusers. Some of the key components of developing a connection and building client engagement are encapsulated in the HARD GOING acronym. The acronym reflects practitioner behaviours and attitudes which can help increase the likelihood that young people will ultimately be prepared to explore options for their own lives.

Honouring	**G**oals of the young person
Active listening	**O**pinions about the young person
Relating	**I**nterpretations of behaviour
Demystifying	**N**egotiations about the process
	Going about it cautiously

Honouring

From the outset, the practitioner fosters a genuine interest in young clients, seeing and valuing them as people separate from their problems. Far from downplaying the significance of their difficulties with school attendance or other problems, this involves honouring them and empathizing with the difficulties they face. Time is spent exploring their interests, concerns and values.

Active listening

From the beginning and throughout, the practitioner employs active listening, allowing the young person to feel heard, understood, accepted and valued. In the process of actively listening, the practitioner learns much about the young person's experiences, motivations and fears, and this information can be used throughout treatment.

Relating

By virtue of the practitioner's role, his/her approach towards the young person may be quite different from that of many other adults in the young person's life. Understandably, some parents, relatives and school personnel may have become annoyed with the young person's school refusal, quite demanding towards the young person and may convey an attitude of having given up on the young person. The practitioner's task, on the other hand, is to relate to the young person in a tolerant, understanding and supportive manner.

Demystifying

The young person's first experience of the helping profession. In other cases, the young person may hold a negative bias towards helpers and the helping profession because of experiences in other settings. For example, while reviewing the previous 'help' received by a 15-year-old girl, she reported that 'one of the last people just sat there and kept repeating stuff I said; it wasn't going anywhere'. Some time is spent demystifying the intervention process, using analogy where helpful. Practitioners may describe themselves as some-what like a driving instructor. While the young person is behind the wheel, controlling what ultimately happens, the practitioner/instructor is available to provide some directions and support along the way.

Goals of the young person

A central goal of intervention is the young person's return to regular voluntary school attendance. This may best be achieved by discovering and attending to other goals that have greater immediate appeal and meaning for the young person. This may include things like making more friends or setting up a computer club at school. In some cases these goals can be addressed simultaneously to the goal of school return. The key element is to identify some things which increase the likelihood that the young person will meet with the practitioner and work towards change.

Opinions about the young person

The practitioner's opinions about the young person will have a large impact on the therapeutic relationship. Thoughts and beliefs that facilitate patience (e.g. 'this young person has had to change schools many times, and needs a lot of support and encouragement in terms of settling into this new school'), tolerance (e.g. 'this young person's oppositional behaviour is reflective of high anxiety about fitting in with others'), hope and respect should be fostered.

Interpretations of behaviour

Efforts to interpret the young person's behaviour, by understanding the meaning behind certain actions or statements, are integral to engagement.

One of the earliest interpretations might be around the young person's apparent disengagement. Refusal to communicate about school issues or to engage in any discussion whatsoever may reflect the young person's extreme annoyance with having parents decide that he/she 'needs help' and must see a practitioner. (For a good discussion on working with children and adolescents who do not readily communicate, see Straus, 1999.) Another young person's frequent and boastful discussion of drug use may be interpreted as a challenge to the practitioner's capacity to be accepting of the young person. Correct interpretations hinge upon a good knowledge of child and adolescent development, together with active listening.

Negotiations about the process

Given that the young person is most unlikely to have elected to participate in an intervention programme, it is advisable that she/he be able to negotiate the process for treatment; for example, the young person may contribute to decision making about how much or how little time is spent in separate sessions or in joint sessions with the parents, or who is seen first. Furthermore, the practitioner continues to check the young person's comfort with aspects of treatment such as role-playing and practice tasks.

Going about it cautiously

Finally, recognizing that the engagement of some young people can be hard going, it is prudent for the practitioner to go about it cautiously, and to have realistic expectations of oneself and of the young person.